Contents

CW01391736

Foreword by Nick Baker

I've been into wildlife and watching it since I was very little and I have learnt the hard way, especially when dealing with the more sensitive creatures, that their ears are much more important to them than perhaps ours are to us.

One jangling zip or a rustle of a rucksack is enough to send even the most lion hearted rabbit running!

So, one of the most important skills for a naturalist is being aware of what every one of your senses are telling you, and also what the senses of all the creatures around you are telling them!

When I'm out with other people showing them how to get close to wildlife and say, for example, a badger has just popped his nose out of his set entrance and is snuffling around, I find myself in a dilemma – I want to talk about it and explain what is going on, but of course this would be a bad idea as the badger would definitely be scared off.

I was doing this exact thing the other day, while in the back of my head thinking about what I would write for Olli's book, when I noticed I was unwittingly signing to the other members of the group. Okay, it was basic and made up on the spot, but the idea was the same – I was talking, but without speaking!

How useful is that! (Olli has certainly inspired me to work on my signing skills. Just imagine having a full conversation without making a noise!)

Signing also has its place in another adventurous occupation of mine, diving. Underwater us divers have a very basic sign language vocabulary that conveys some of the most basic, but important, situations and problems.

I remember taking some deaf friends diving with great white sharks, and while I could only sit there in a bubbly silence, these two friends, who are both shark watching enthusiasts, were having a full blown conversation about how excited this was making them feel, the colour of the shark, its teeth, and that there was another one behind me!!

It was an amazing thing to see.

Both of these experiences have taught me that learning to sign has a very cool and important role to play when studying nature.

Thank you, Olli, for opening my eyes, (literally), to a skill that I had overlooked until now.

Happy nature watching!

Nick
Nick Baker, Television Naturalist

> **Olli has certainly inspired me to work on my signing skills. Just imagine having a full conversation without making a noise!**

Introduction by **Garry Slack**

Welcome to 'Learn to sign about nature with Olli'.

This book will help children of all ages to improve their communication skills through the use of sign language and will stimulate an interest in wildlife and the natural world.

Whether they have access to the countryside, a garden, or live in a more urban environment, children will be able to learn more about sign language and their environment through a series of fun packed, practical projects.

Olli Says:
My Grandad says that in a lifetime, the average human being eats eight spiders while they are sleeping! ......I'm not sure if he is joking, but after hearing that, I'm glad that I'm a monkey!

Why learn to sign about nature?

Whoever you are and whatever country you may live in, whether you live in a large British city or in a tiny African village, each and every one of us are united by two things.

Firstly, by the planet that we call home – The Earth, and secondly by our instinctive desire to communicate with one another.

In parts of Europe there are fabulous cave paintings of wild animals that are over thirty thousand years old. The meaning behind these paintings is not known. They may have been for decoration or perhaps they showed some kind of ceremony. Whatever the meaning of these prehistoric images, it is clear that mankind and nature have a relationship with one another that stretches back for centuries.

In more modern times we still share our ancestors' fascination of the natural world. Whether it's watching a bird collecting twigs to build a nest in spring time or gathering together at a window to watch the raindrops pounding the window pane during a particularly heavy rain storm - nature still has the power to amaze and enthral us.

In fact, in Britain nature is the inspiration for one of our main topics of conversation – the weather. Hardly surprising when we live in a country with such a variable climate.

The changing seasons make us all aware of the natural cycle of life. Plants grow, flower, set seed and die. Animals too follow a similar pattern.

Just like the animals and plants, our lives are also influenced by nature.

Both the weather and our surroundings can affect how we feel. I'm sure that you have heard people say that they are 'full of the joys of spring' or that they are 'feeling under the weather'. From time to time we all talk of 'getting away from it all' and 'getting back to nature'.

Although many of us now live in urban areas, more and more people are increasingly becoming aware that as human beings we are in fact part of nature, not separate from it. Every person, plant, animal and living thing is connected to and dependant on each other in order to survive.

The natural world and green issues are now classed by governments and local authorities as a 'high priority' topic. Everyone seems to agree that we need to reconnect with nature and preserve our precious planet.

Throughout the world people are doing their bit to help wildlife and the environment. But conservation isn't just about saving the rainforests and oceans – it also means caring for our immediate surroundings and the plants and animals that share our cities, towns, villages and even the streets where we live.

In order for the Earth and all its inhabitants to flourish and survive we need to work together to nurture and cherish our planet. This means communicating with one another to share our thoughts and ideas.

Good communication skills enable us to connect with one another, to grow friendships and to build strong, healthy relationships.

Sign language is perhaps, alongside cave paintings, one of our oldest forms of communication. The signs in this book are simple and straightforward to learn which makes learning to sign a more enjoyable experience. In no time a child can be using the signs to increase their vocabulary of signs and develop their language skills.

This book will help all children to learn more about nature and what they can do to help look after their environment, whilst enabling them to communicate effectively using fun, easy to learn signs sourced directly from British Sign Language.

Get out there and discover a whole new world!

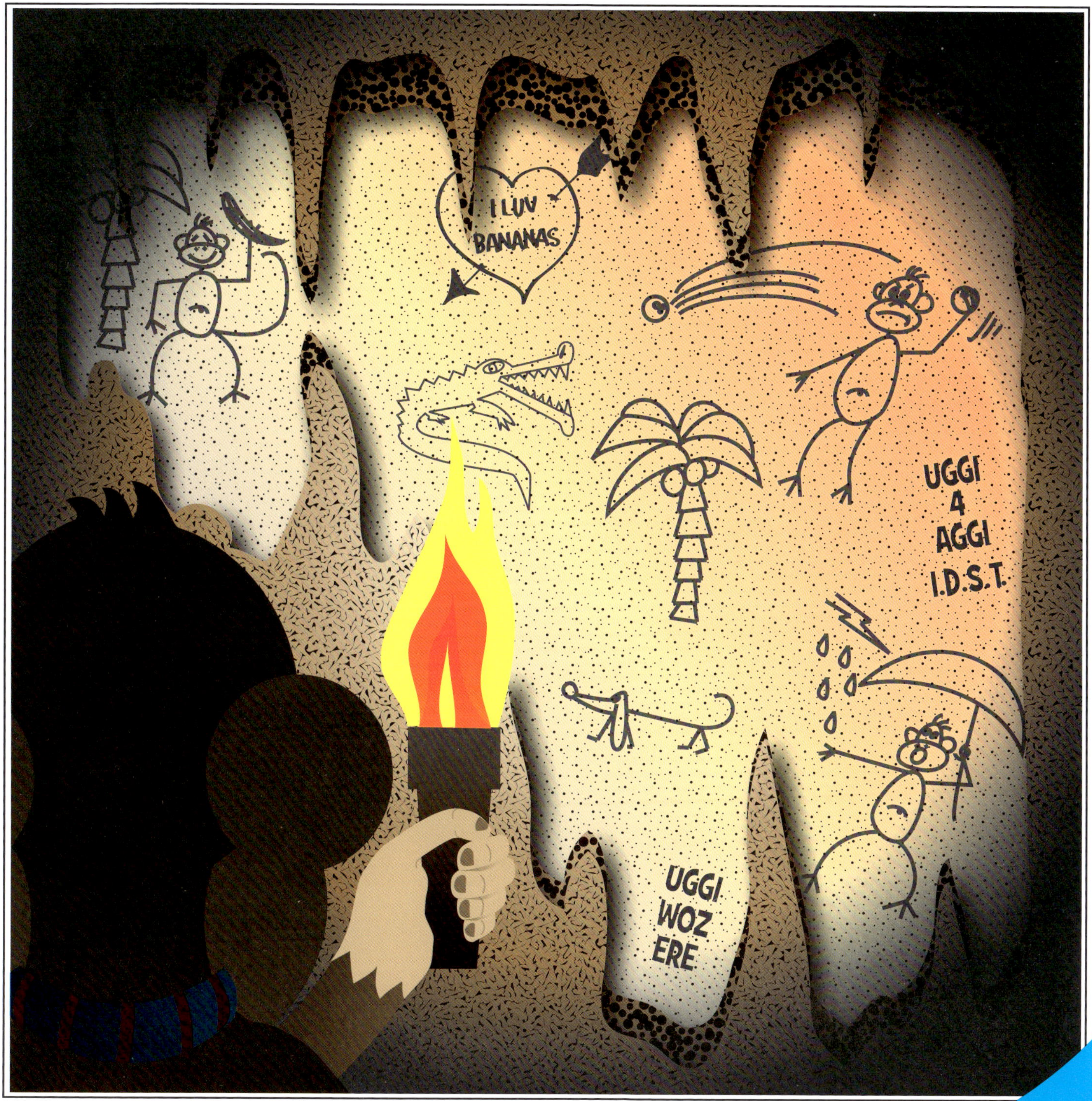
I LUV BANANAS
UGGI 4 AGGI I.D.S.T.
UGGI WOZ ERE

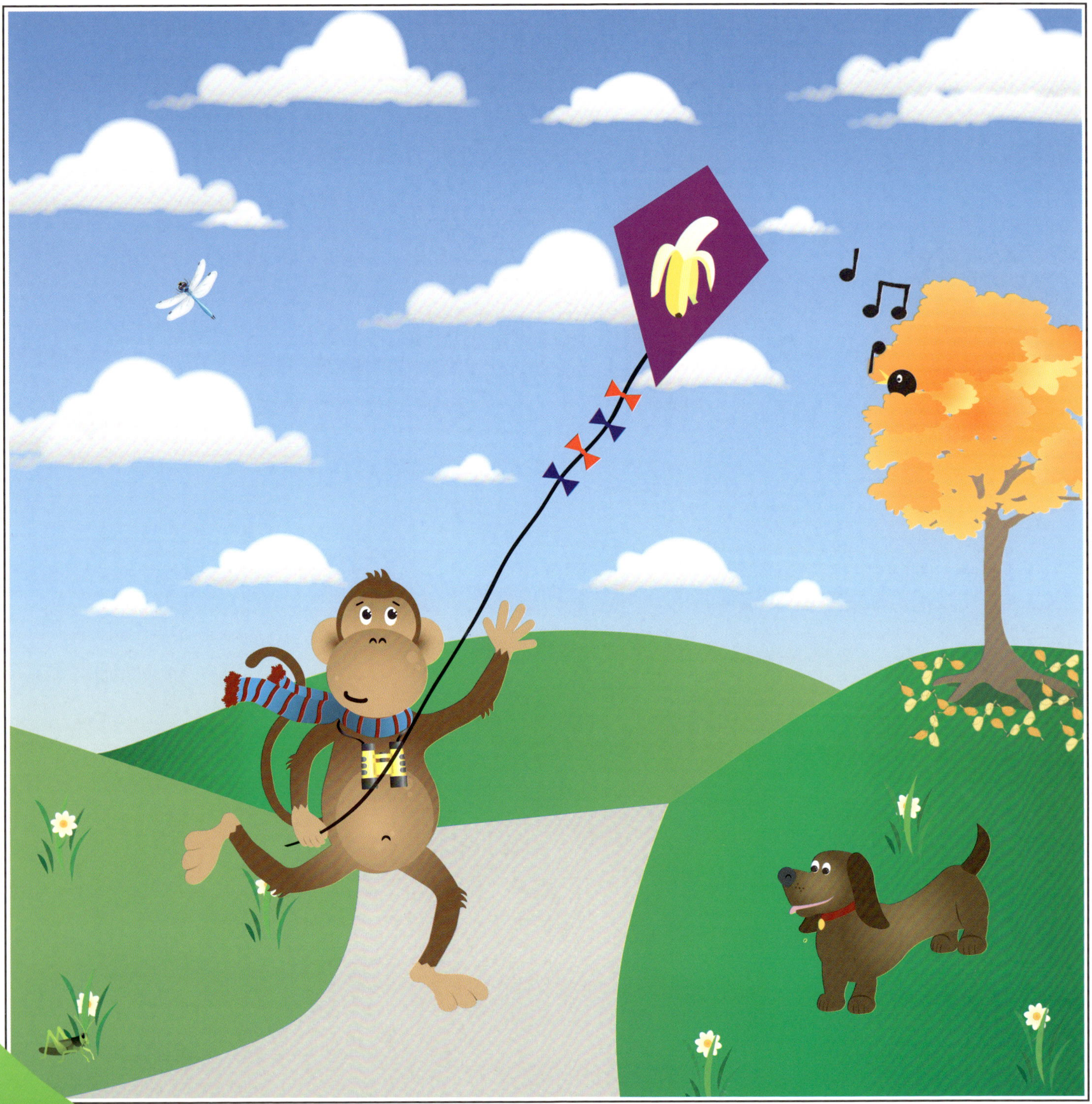

Benefits of learning to sign about nature

Increases communication skills

By introducing new signs based around the themes of wildlife and nature, this book helps to build on a child's existing knowledge of sign language.

This will help to expand their vocabulary of signs and increase their communication skills.

Good communication skills are so important because they allow a child to build relationships with others and take a full and active role in society.

Stimulates an interest in the natural world and the environment

Many children are often amazed at just how close the natural world is to them. Finding a feather in a local park or seeing a group of rabbits feeding on the grass verge by a busy road can often spark an interest in nature. These chance encounters inevitably lead to questions such as, 'what kind of bird is this feather from?' or 'where do the rabbits live?'

This is a great opportunity to encourage a child to discover more about the plants and animals that share our surroundings.

This curiosity to find out more about wildlife can help children to realise their own connection with nature and their role and responsibility in making sure that the environment is well cared for to benefit all living things.

Raises an awareness of the seasons and the life cycles of living things

Learning about nature helps children to learn that every living thing on our planet, whether it is a plant, a human being or a frog, goes through the same life processes.

Through learning about nature, children learn about the cycle of life from birth to death and how all animals and plants rely on each other to survive.

Just growing a plant such as a sunflower from seed teaches a child that things need to be looked after and cared for so that they can grow, flower and produce new seeds to make other plants.

Beneficial to health

Nowadays a lot of people worry that many children spend far too much time indoors playing computer games or watching television.

Being encouraged to play outdoors means that a child is not only interacting with their environment, but they are also gaining the benefits of fresh air and exercise.

Playing outside is not only good for physical health, since it often involves activities such as walking, running or even climbing trees, but it is also good for developing problem solving skills, whether it is identifying a bird or plant by using a nature book or working out the best way to build a den.

A hobby for life

Developing an interest in nature can literally become a lifetime hobby.

A lot of the famous naturalists that we see on the TV started out by exploring their own back gardens.

Nature is such a huge subject, covering not only things like bird watching or animal tracking, but also looking after the environment and even gardening.

The best news of all is that unlike some other hobbies, it's incredibly cheap.... In fact, it's very often free!

Even those without a garden can grow their own plants and vegetables, all of which is good for both wildlife and the environment. Growing plants from seed is very cheap and the plants can be given as gifts.

Because of their different characteristics, such as the way they smell, feel and move in the breeze, plants can help to stimulate all the senses and are great for creating sensory gardens for children who may have special needs.

The different textures, colours and smells will be great for helping them to explore and enjoy the environment.

Helps to develop physical and practical skills

Activities such as learning sign language and gardening help to develop physical skills such as hand-eye coordination and help to develop a child's fine motor skills. These are essential abilities that children will need to master in order to control items such as pens and pencils.

By taking part in practical projects, like making a bird table or measuring rainfall, children will learn essential life skills such as numeracy, literacy and problem solving.

Learning is fun!

The best way to learn about nature is to get out into the great outdoors and experience it at first hand.

There is no substitute for seeing and experiencing things for yourself, even if it does mean getting a bit messy from time to time. Actually, for most children that's probably half the fun.

Don't worry about getting your hands dirty, you should always wash them afterwards anyway. Just get out there and explore!

How to **use this book**

A lot of people who are new to learning sign language are often overwhelmed by the number of signs contained in many of the more traditional, 'dictionary' style sign language books that are on the market.
To enable you to learn the signs in manageable 'chunks', this book is divided into different sections.

The signs in the book are grouped together into related categories. For example, signs like 'river' or 'waterfall' can be found in the 'Signs for the natural world' section, whilst the signs for animals such as 'fox' or 'bat' are to be found in, 'Beast, Bugs & Birds'.

The book also contains practical projects that children can do and make throughout the four seasons of the year.
These projects will help to engage and encourage children to interact with nature, whilst they learn the signs associated with each season.

How to learn the signs
To produce any of the signs in the book, begin by looking at the picture and copy the positions and shapes of the hands, arms, body and facial expressions.
Read the description which explains how to perform the sign.
Arrows on some of the pictures help you to see how the hands should move and in which direction.

All of the photographs and descriptions in this book are shown and described from a right handed person's perspective. If you are left handed simply reverse the instructions.

Hand shapes

Sometimes it can be difficult to describe in a book how a particular sign is made or in what position the hands should be. To make it easier for you to produce a sign there are several common hand shapes that occur frequently in sign language.

When you are looking at the vocabulary pages you may notice that sometimes they refer to a "Full C hand" or a "Bunched hand" Whenever you see these, or any other hand shapes referred to, use the pictures below to help you to produce the sign accurately.

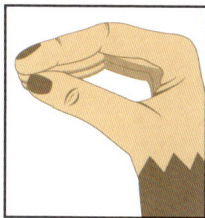

Bent Hand

Bunched Hand

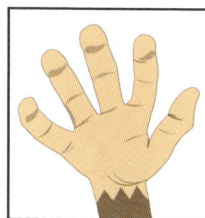

'C' Hand

Clawed Hand

Closed Hand

Shell
Both 'Clawed' hands, one on top of the other, with palms facing, open and close like a clam.

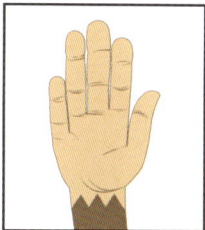

Fist

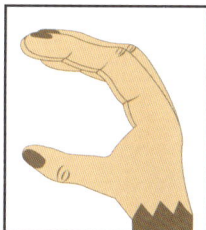

Flat Hand

Full 'C' Hand

'M' Hand

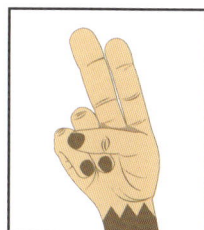

'N' Hand

Above is an example of how signs are presented in the vocabulary sections of the book. The direction of movement is shown by the red arrows on the vocabulary pictures. Double arrowheads indicate where two repeat movements are required.

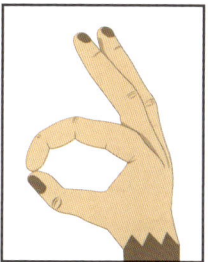

'O' Hand

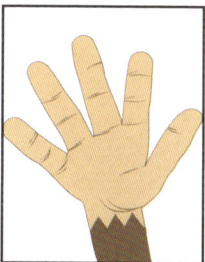

Open Hand

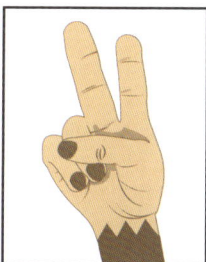

'V' Hand

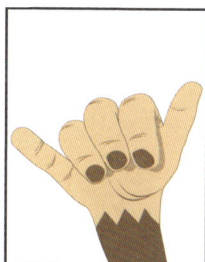

'Y' Hand

Finger Spelling

Finger spelling is the backbone of sign language. In British Sign Language, both hands are used to create the 26 letters of the alphabet. Finger spelling can be used to spell the names of people, places and objects.

Here is how a right handed person would sign the alphabet from A to Z. Notice how the index and other fingers of the right hand spell out the letters on the left hand or point to the vowels on the opposite fingers.

If you are left handed, simply reverse this process and lead with your left hand.

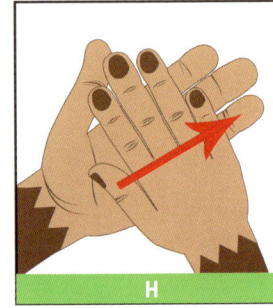

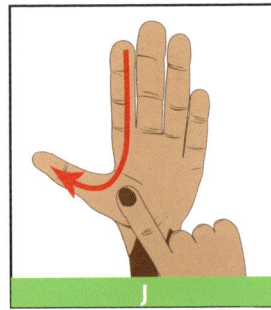

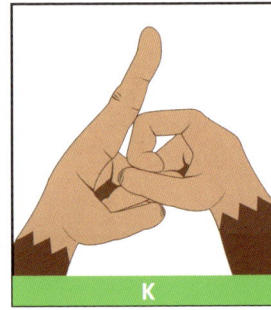

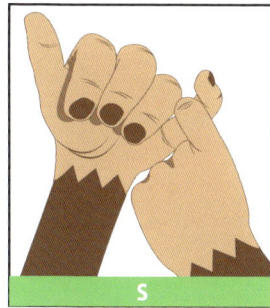

M

N

O

P

Q

R

S

T

U

V

W

X

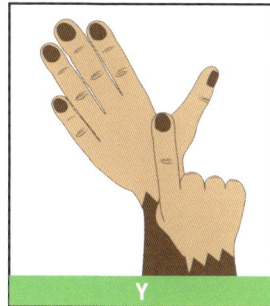

Y

Z

Signs for the calendar

It's easy to sign the months of the year - just use your fingers to spell out the letters of each month.
In the same way that you sometimes shorten a long word when you are texting a friend, you sometimes only need to spell out a few key letters of those months that have lots of letters in their names.

JAN

The month of January gets its name from the Roman God, Janus. Janus had two faces, which meant he could look back on the old year, and at the same time see forward into the year that lay ahead.

In Britain the weather in January can be really cold. In fact, in 1814 it was so cold in London that the river Thames froze! The ice was so thick that the citizens held a special 'Frost Fair' on the ice with stalls, dancing and entertainment.

FEB

February is the shortest month of the year and usually has only twenty eight days, unless it's a leap year, when there are twenty nine.

Does that mean if you are born on the twenty ninth of February that you only have a birthday every four years?

MAR

The third month of the year is named after Mars, the Roman god of war.

Folklore says that the weather in March 'Comes in like a lion and goes out like a lamb'.

I've never seen a lion in March, but it can certainly be a very blustery month!

APR

(Finger spell the letter 'A', twice)

The first of April is traditionally when people play jokes and tricks on one another. Some people love to fool their friends and neighbours with silly jokes, but unless the prank takes place before midday, the joke is on them!

MAY

May is the time for fun and flowers!

For centuries in Britain people have greeted the first day of May with dancing and special celebrations. The parties were to celebrate the passing of winter and the coming of summer. Many villages even had a special pole called a Maypole that the villagers would dance around to encourage the nature spirits to bring them good luck.

JUN

(Finger spell the letters J U N E)

June is named after the Roman goddess of marriage, Junno, so maybe that's why so many people get married in June!

June is the start of summer in the Northern Hemisphere and on 21st June, the longest day of the year, people gather at Stonehenge to celebrate the Summer Solstice.

JUL

(Finger spell the letters J U L Y)

July is named after the Roman Emperor, Julius Caesar and it is usually one of the hottest months of the year. But legend says that if it rains on St Swithin's Day, on July 15th then it will rain non stop for forty days!

For me though, the best thing about July is the start of the summer holidays!

AUG

August is the eighth month of the year and is named in honour of the Roman Emperor, Augustus Caesar, (those Romans seem to have really liked naming the months of the year after their Emperors and Gods!)

SEP

(Or just finger spell the letter 'S', if you want to be really fast!)

In the calendar that we use today, September is the ninth month of the year, but in fact the name September comes from the ancient Roman word, 'Septem' which means' seven'. (Yep, it's those Romans again!). Septem was the seventh month in their calendar. For me, September means the end of the summer and that it's time to go back to school!

OCT

I bet you can't guess how October got its name?

No, it wasn't named after an Octopus! But there is a clue there. 'Octo' means 'eight' in the language used by the Romans. This was because October was the eighth month of the Roman year.

NOV

The weather in this month can be dark and miserable, so maybe that is why there are so many bright and colourful celebrations in November.
People in Britain celebrate Guy Fawkes Night on November the 5th, the anniversary of the Gunpowder Plot, while in the United States of America families gather together to celebrate Thanksgiving on the fourth Thursday in November.
November is named after 'Novem', the Roman word for the number nine.

DEC

No prizes for guessing who gave December its name! December was the tenth month of the Roman calendar.

For us in the Northern Hemisphere it's the start of winter.

December 21st is the Winter Solstice – the shortest day of the year.

Fast Fingers!

How fast do you think you can finger spell? Challenge your friends to a finger spelling race and see who has the fastest fingers!

Practise finger spelling each of the twelve months that make up the calendar. Start slowly at first, then gradually build up your speed and see how quickly you can spell out each name.

With a bit of practise, you will soon be a champion finger speller like me!

While you are improving your finger spelling, why not astound your friends with how much you know about the months of the year? It's amazing how many of the names of the months that we use today originally came from ancient Rome!

Whatever the weather

**Thunder, snow,
fog and drizzle
or sun that makes the
pavements sizzle.
Whatever the forecast,
let's all together,
learn to sign
about the weather!**

In the modern world finding out what the weather is going to be like is so easy. One flick of the TV remote control or click of the mouse to log onto a website, is all it takes. But in the old days, before television weather presenters or the internet came along, people relied on nature to help them forecast the weather.

Many of us now live in towns and cities and buy our food from supermarkets, but in the past people farmed the land and grew their own food.
This meant that the weather was a very important part of people's lives.
Good weather meant a good harvest, but a drought, or a long spell of rain, could be a disaster for the farmers and their families.

Before modern scientific ways of forecasting the weather were invented, using satellites and computers, people would look for signs in the skies and in the behaviour of animals and plants to help them predict the weather.

To help them remember what the different skies and weather patterns meant, people would make up rhymes and sayings such as, 'Red sky at night, shepherds delight' or 'Rain before seven, fine by eleven'.

As well as looking at the changing skies, animals were also used to predict the weather. It was thought that animals would behave unusually if a storm was approaching.
Bees would go back to the hive, cows would lie down or huddle together, spiders would leave their webs and dogs would appear jumpy and nervous, whilst cats were thought to groom themselves and meow more.

People didn't just rely on animals to predict the weather. Many plants are great at forecasting the weather too. For example, daisies are very sensitive to changes in the weather. If the weather is fine then they will fully open their flowers, but if it threatens to rain then their flowers will shut tight.

Another traditional way of predicting the weather is to use pine cones.

Pine cones react to the amount of water that is in the air. If the weather is fine then the pine cones will open up because the air is dry. Damp air will make the cones close up, and you will know that rain is on the way. Pine cones are easy to find and much cheaper than buying an expensive barometer.

My Grandma claims to be able to predict the weather too. She says that she can always tell when it is going to rain because she can feel it in her bones!

Whatever the weather might be like, it's important that when you go out you are wearing the right clothing to protect you from the elements. In fact, my Grandma says that there is no such thing as bad weather! She often tells me that 'The weather is always right, but sometimes our clothes are wrong!'

To help you know what to wear when you go out on safari, I've managed to persuade my brother Iggi to model some of the right clothes for you.

Hey Iggi, The cows are lying down........don't forget your umbrella!

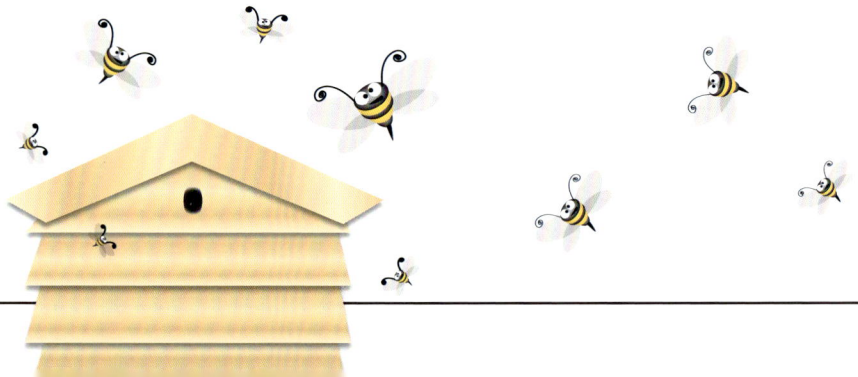

Whether the weather be hot,
or whether the weather be not,
we'll weather the weather,
whatever the weather,
whether we like it or not!

SPRING & SUMMER

AUTUMN & WINTER

Olli says:
Did you know that in August 1997 the zookeepers at Edinburgh Zoo had to put sun tan lotion on the penguins because the weather was so hot that the penguins had started to lose their feathers!

Signs for the weather - Vocabulary

Breeze / Cool
Fan your face gently with both 'Flat' hands, palms facing towards your face.

Cloud / Cloudy
Both 'Clawed' hands, with the palms facing away from you, make alternate small circular movements just slightly above your head.

Dark / Night
With both hands flat, pointing upwards and the palms facing towards you, swing your hands downwards so that they cross each other and end up across your body at waist height.

Dry
Hold both 'Bunched' hands, with fingertips pointing upwards, and rub the tips of your thumbs across the pads of your fingertips, starting from the little fingers across to the index fingers.

Fog / Mist
Both 'Open' hands, with the palms facing away from you, make slow, alternate, circular movements in front of your face.

Hot
'Clawed' hand moves across the mouth from left to right.

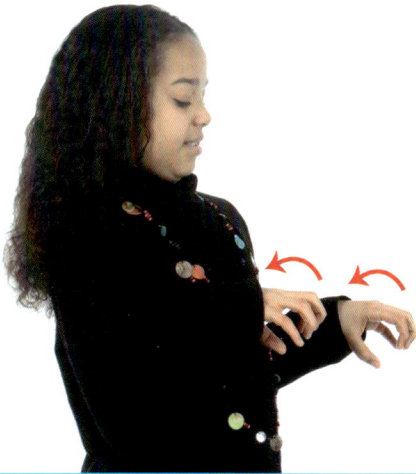

Frost / Ice / Freeze / Icy
Hold both hands in front of you with the palms facing downwards. Move them backwards sharply towards your body into 'Clawed' hand shapes, as if clawing ice.

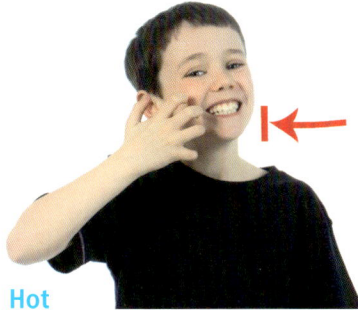

Light / Dawn / Day
Start with both arms crossed, with the palms facing towards your body at waist height. Now swing your hands upwards so that they cross each other and end up at either side of your face.

Lightning
Index finger moves downwards sharply, in a zig – zag, to show the shape of a lightning strike.

Melt
Hold both 'Open' hands, with palms facing each other. Move both hands slowly apart, whilst at the same time rubbing the tips of your thumbs across the pads of your fingertips, starting from the little fingers across to the index fingers. Finish so that your hands are both apart with the palms facing upwards.

Rainbow
Full 'C' hand describes the shape of a rainbow in a large arc above the head.

Rain
Hold both 'Open' hands, with the palms facing downwards. Move them downwards twice, wiggling the fingers to show gentle rain. To show heavy rain, puff out your cheeks and move your hands downwards several times more forcefully.

Storm / Gale
Both 'Flat' hands, with palms facing each other, are held in front of your head. Move them from side to side as if they were being blown about in a gale.

Sunrise / Sunset
Show the action of the Sun rising by moving a full 'O' hand up from behind the left arm which is held across the front of the body. As your right hand gets to the vertical position, show the rays of the Sun by opening the fingers of your hand.
To show 'Sunset', reverse this action.

Sun / Sunny
Look up at a raised 'Bunched' hand which then springs open, like the rays of the Sun.

Temperature
Hold up your left index finger and then move your right index finger up and down it to show the rise and fall of the line in a thermometer.

Thunder (Two part sign)
Make the sign for 'Lightning' (P 17) and then hold both 'Open' hands, with palms facing downwards, and shake them from side to side a few times.

Weather
One 'Open' hand, with the palm facing your face, makes two short movements towards you.

Wet / Damp
Open and close the fingers of both 'Bunched' hands a few times.

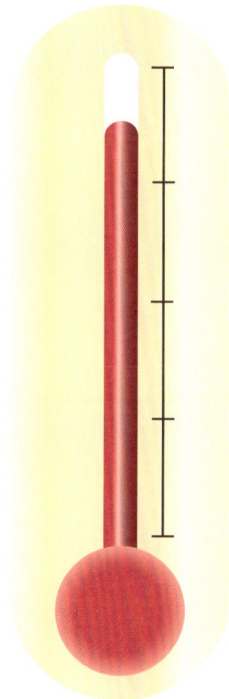

Wind
Puff out your cheeks and fan your face strongly several times with both 'Open' hands, palms facing towards your face.

19

Go Green, Gabbi Gibbon!

Meet my cousin, Gabbi Gibbon, and her family. They are always in a hurry, but is their lifestyle harming the environment?

Let's see what a typical day with the Gibbon family is like.

Can you spot anything that they could do to have a greener lifestyle?

Gabbi's in the bathroom getting ready for school...

... Meanwhile, in the kitchen, Gabbi's Dad is preparing his lunch.

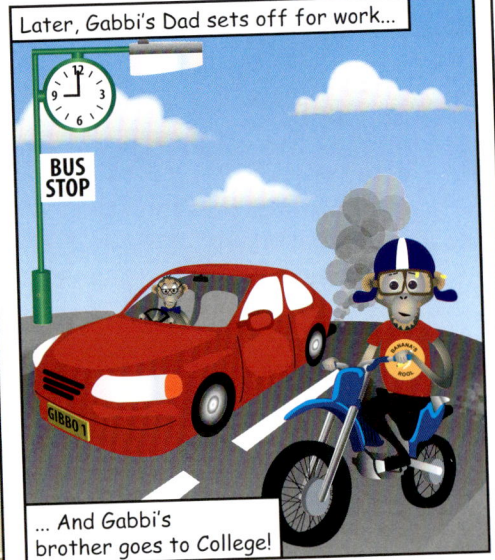

Later, Gabbi's Dad sets off for work...

... And Gabbi's brother goes to College!

Lunchtime & Gabbi's Mum's in the office...

...Gabbi's brother is at Croco Burgers!

Dad gets the shopping on the way home!

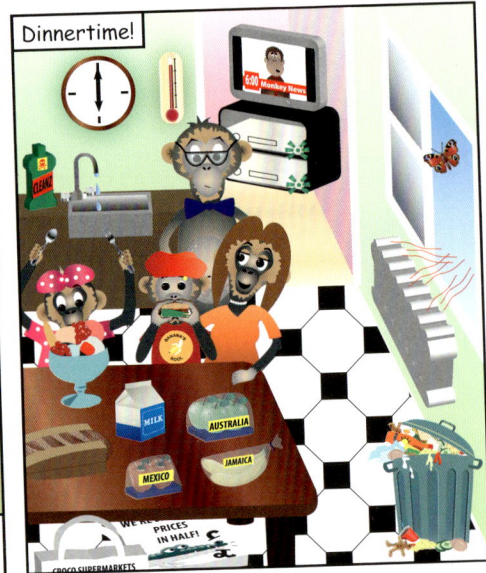

Dinnertime!

The Gibbons' lead really busy lives and their house is full of all the latest hi – tech gadgets, but sometimes they don't always think about how the way that they live can affect the environment.

I'm sure that with just a little help, Gabbi and her family could become a little bit greener.

We all share the same planet so it's really important that we look after our world.
Each of us can do our bit to help, by saving energy and cutting down on the amount of waste that we all produce everyday.

Here are a few ways that will help you to do your bit for our planet:

- **Save water, take a shower** - You will not only save water but energy too because a shower uses less hot water. Remember to turn off any dripping taps. A dripping tap can waste up to 90 litres of water everyday.

- **Unplug any unnecessary electrical appliances that are not in use** - Some electrical products can't be switched off completely unless they are unplugged. Items that are left on standby continue to draw power twenty four hours a day. These products are known as 'energy vampires'.

- **Don't leave your PC or TV on standby** - A PC or TV uses 90% of the energy on standby as they would if fully turned on. This wasted power not only costs lots of money but it can also help to damage the planet by creating carbon dioxide which adds to climate change.

- **Get on your bike!** - Riding a bike or walking is not only fun but it's kinder to the environment. If it's too far to walk or cycle, hop on a bus or train.

- **Bin it!** - Don't leave your litter lying about for someone else to pick up. If you can't find a bin nearby, take your rubbish home and see if it can be recycled.

- **Watch your waste!** - Try to get everyone in your family to cut down the amount of things that you throw away. Fruit and vegetable peelings can be put on a compost heap. Newspapers, magazines, tin cans and glass bottles can be sent for recycling. Clothes that you no longer wear can be sent to charity shops or cut up and used as rags for cleaning. Encourage who ever does the shopping in your house to buy products made with recycled material and ask them to buy shampoos and cleaning products that contain natural herbs, rather than chemicals that may harm the environment.

- **Don't press print!** – Print things from your PC only when you really need to. If you have to print, use both sides of the paper.

- **Use a sandwich box** – Rather than wrap your sandwiches in cling film, put your lunch in a sandwich box that can be used again and again.

- **Be a smart shopper!** - Take your own bags to the supermarket and watch out for any unnecessary packaging. Try to buy things like fruit and vegetables loose. Some foods are flown half way around the world before they end up on your plate. Buying food that is produced locally will cut down on the air miles.

- **Turn down the heat** – If the thermostat for the central heating in your house is set higher than 20°C, ask if it can be turned down. You can always wear a sweater if it gets chilly! Turning down the thermostat just a bit can help to save money.

Olli says:
Did you know that every year the UK produces more than 300 million tonnes of waste, a quarter of this waste comes from homes and businesses!

Signs for the natural world -
Vocabulary

Beach
Hold both hands together in front of your body and rub the tips of the thumbs, index and middle fingers together as if you were rubbing grains of sand through your fingertips. Move your hands apart in opposite directions.

Branch
Hold up your left hand with the palm facing away from you and the fingers spread apart, to represent a tree. Make your right hand into a 'C' hand shape next to the thumb of your left hand, then move it away in a curve to show the outline of a branch.

Bush
Use 'Clawed' hands, with the palms facing forwards, to describe the shape of a bush.

Countryside / Field / Meadow
The 'Flat' right hand, with palm facing downwards, sweeps up the outstretched right arm from the wrist towards the elbow.

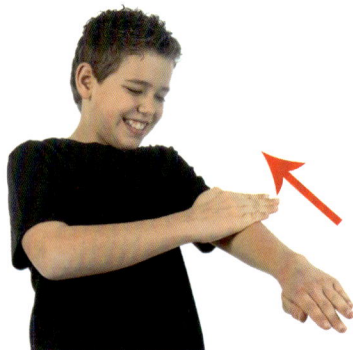

Environment
Left hand in a fist, with the index finger pointing upwards is held in front of the body. The 'Open' right hand, with palm facing downwards, moves in circles above the left index finger, whilst wiggling the fingers at the same time.

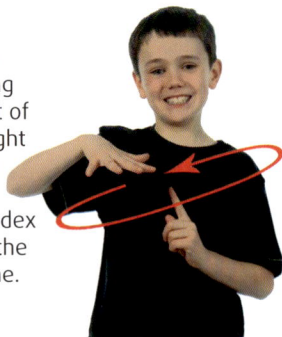

Cliff
Hold both 'Flat' hands, side by side in front of you to show the top of the cliff. Twist your right hand and move it sharply downwards, twisting back and forth slightly at the wrist, to show the rough cliff face.

Flower
'Sniff' an imaginary flower by holding a right 'O' shaped hand under each nostril in turn.

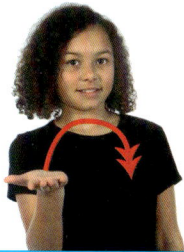

Garden

'Flat' hand, with palm facing upwards, moves slightly forwards away from the body, flipping over to palm facing downwards a few times in a 'digging' action to show the turning over of the soil.

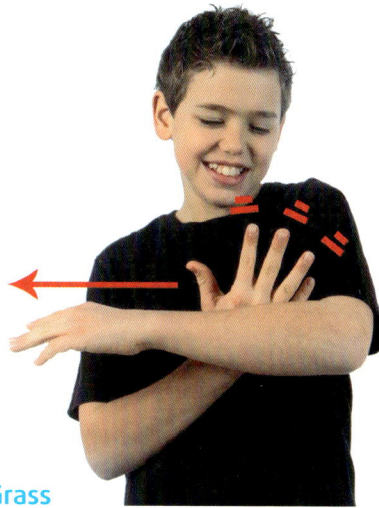

Grass

The left forearm is held in front of the body, whilst the wiggling fingers of the right hand, representing the blades of grass, move along behind the left arm.

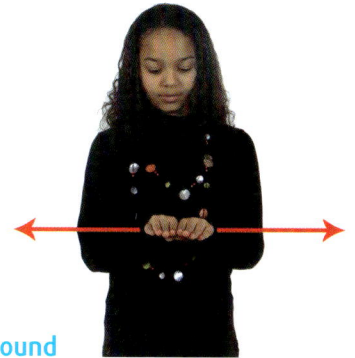

Ground

Both 'Flat' hands, with palms facing downwards, are held together in front of the body at waist height. Move the hands apart from each other.

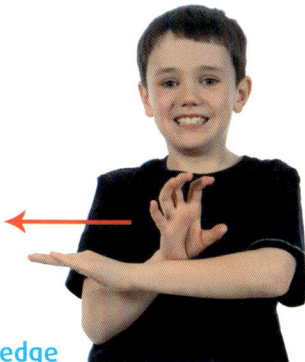

Hedge

The left forearm is held in front of the body, whilst a 'Clawed' right hand, with palm facing forwards, moves along behind the left arm, to show the line of the 'hedge'.

Hill

Use your 'Flat' hand, with palm facing downwards, to describe the outline of the shape of a hill.

Lake / Pond

'Flat' hand, with palm facing downwards, outlines the shape of the lake or pond, while the fingers wiggle to imitate the rippling of the water. (Will vary according to the size of the lake or pond that you are describing).

Land

'Open' hand, with palm facing downwards, moves away and back towards the body in an arc.

Leaf

Starting from the tip of the left index finger, use the index finger and thumb of the other hand to open and close, describing the outline and shape of a leaf.

Mountain

Describe the shape of a mountain by having both 'Flat' hands, with palms facing each other, move upwards and towards each other, twisting slightly at the wrists, until the fingertips are touching.

Nature / Natural

Finger spell the letter 'N' twice.

Nature Reserve (Two part sign)

Start by making the sign for 'Land' (P 23), then the blade of right 'Flat' hand sweeps back towards you across the palm of the left hand to sign 'Reserve'.

Ocean / Sea

Both 'Open' hands, with palms facing downwards, move up and down and apart from each other to show the waves of the sea.

River / Stream

Two 'N' hands held slightly apart, with palms facing each other, move forwards and away from the body, weaving from side to side to show the twists and turns of the path of a river.

Rock

Both 'Clawed' hands are held in front of the body facing each other, as if holding a rock. The right hand twists forwards slightly.

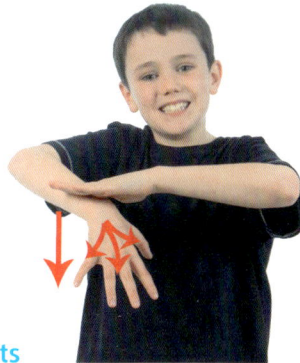

Roots

Hold your left 'Flat' hand, with palm facing downwards to represent the ground. Hold your other hand underneath in a full 'O' shape and then open your fingers to show the shape of the roots of a plant or tree.

Sand

Rub the tips of the thumb, index and middle fingers together as your hands move upwards, as if you were rubbing grains of sand through your fingertips.

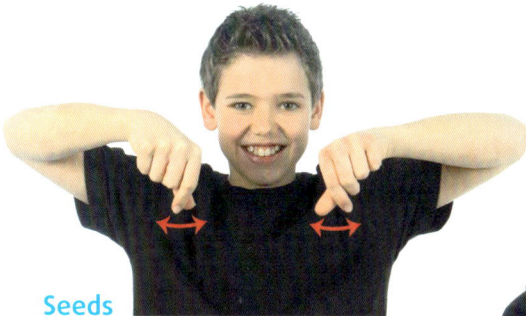

Seeds

Rub the tips of the thumbs and index fingers together.

Soil

Hold both 'Bunched' hands, with palms facing downwards, and rub the tips of the thumbs twice across the back of the fingertips.

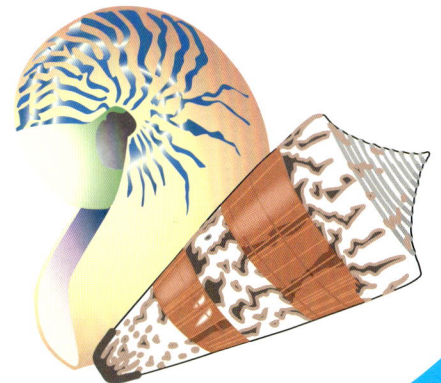

Sky

Hold both hands above the head, with the palms facing downwards and move them slowly apart whilst looking up to the sky.

Shell

Both 'Clawed' hands, one on top of the other, with palms facing, open and close like a clam.

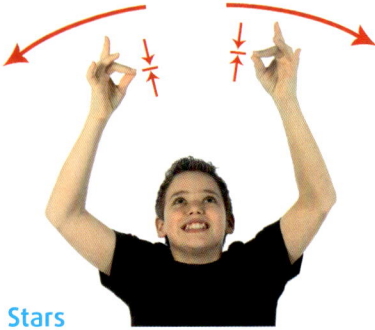

Stars

Both hands are held above the head. The middle fingers of both hands open and close against the thumbs as the hands move apart.

Stone

'Clawed' right hand, facing left, twists slightly forwards above the extended index finger of the left hand.

Tree / Forest / Woods

To show a single Tree, the elbow of the right arm rests on the back of the left hand. The fingers of the right hand represent the branches of a tree. To sign 'Forest' or 'Wood', the whole shape then moves slightly to the right and forwards in an arc, to indicate more than one tree.

Valley

Both 'Flat' hands, with palms facing, are held at shoulder height. Move your hands downwards towards each other to describe the shape of a valley.

Water

With an 'O' hand, brush the index finger and thumb down the cheek, twice.

Waterfall

Both 'Open' hands, with palms facing downwards and fingers wiggling, move downwards and slightly off to the side, before levelling off again, to show the shape and movement of a waterfall.

The World / Planet

Both 'Open' hands describe the circular shape of the world.

The Animal Alphabet Song

A – B – C - D and E
See the bird in the apple tree
F – G – H - I and J
Rabbit, deer and the fox at play
K - L - M - N - O - P - Q
A snake, a spider and a hedgehog too
R – S – T - U and V
Fish are swimming in the sea
W - X - Y and Z
The badger and the bat say it's time for bed

Signs of spring

Flying a kite on a windy day, lighter nights and mad March Hares!

The winter snows begin to melt away and gradually the days get longer and warmer.
New shoots push their way up out of the soil. Daffodils, crocuses and snowdrops appear and the buds on the trees begin to burst.

Spring is full of activity as hibernating animals wake up from their long winter sleep and start searching for food. Birds are busy building nests and feeding on the insects that crawl out from their winter hiding places.

Out in the countryside, you might be able to spot a brown hare dashing through a farmer's field. Brown hares are the fastest land animals in the UK and can run at speeds of up to forty five miles per hour.

Olli's Forecast

Expect the unexpected!

Frosty nights, warm, sunny days, showers, rainbows, hailstones, floods and sometimes even snow. When it comes to the weather in spring time, almost anything can happen!

Hold tightly onto your coats and hats in the blustery March winds. And don't forget your umbrella to shield you from those famous April showers. Sometimes the weather in early spring is strictly for the ducks!

Mind you, I love putting my Wellies on and having a splashing time in all those puddles. Just remember that although we sometimes grumble when it rains, every plant and animal needs water to live.
So, don't complain about the rain, get out there, get wet and have fun!

It might be wet and windy now, but as May approaches it will soon start to get warmer...summer is nearly here!

Look Out For:

Things that hop....

The warmer weather of spring means that even the frogs, which have been in hibernation all winter, are on the move, looking for a suitable place to spawn. Who knows, they may even be hopping to a pond near you!

If you go outside with a torch on a warm, soggy spring night, you might see frogs in and around the pond.

Frogs are great for your garden because they will eat invertebrates, (things without a backbone), such as slugs and snails.

If a frog hops into your house then it is meant to be a sign of good luck.

In the old days it was even believed that frogs could predict the weather!

'A frog that croaks throughout the day, means that rain is on the way'

Things that flap....

As the weather warms up, bats come out of hibernation and are in need of a good meal.

The best time to see them is when it gets dark when they are out searching for food.

Some people are scared of bats, but don't believe all the stuff you see in the movies about giant, blood drinking bats!

British bats are small and only eat insects. In fact, a bat can eat half its own weight in insects in just one night.

The smallest British bat is called a pipistrelle. At only four centimetres in length and weighing no more than a pound coin, the pipistrelle bat is so small that it could easily fit into a matchbox.

Even the largest British bat, the noctule, is only about twice that size and weighs up to 40 grams.
Not really frightening enough to give you nightmares are they?!

It's true that in some parts of the world there are giant bats, and some of them, like the vampire bat, really do drink blood.

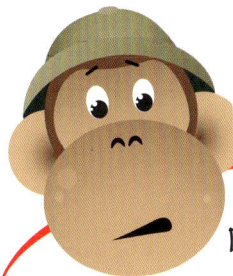

The largest bat in the world is called the Javanese Flying Fox which has a wingspan of almost two metres.

Relax though because it lives in South East Asia and eats fruit!

Many bats in the UK are at risk because there are fewer places for them to roost and less insects for them to feed on.

You could help bats by putting up a bat box for them to roost in and encouraging more insects into your garden for them to feed on.

Simple things like putting on an outside light for a few minutes in the early evening will attract flying insects such as moths and provide the bats with a tasty meal.

Olli says:
Did you know that frogs don't need to drink? When they are in a pond and get thirsty, they just soak up all the water that they need through their skin – that's a bit like you drinking your own bathwater when you fancy a drink!

Things on the wing.....

Spring is a really busy time for birds.

In early spring you will be able to see birds such as blackbirds, sparrows and starlings collecting things to make their nests with. You can help them by putting out nesting material such as straw, the fluff from the tumble dryer or even pet fur!

By May the nests should be full of hungry baby birds and the adults will be out hunting for food for the chicks.

To encourage birds into your garden don't be too tidy. Birds hunt for insects in piles of leaves and dead plants, so allow a corner of your garden to become a little wild.

Watch the skies too because spring is when many birds begin to arrive from overseas. These birds are called migrants. They have flown thousands of miles to spend the summer here.

The swift is a migrant bird which visits the UK each summer from Africa. Swifts are fantastic fliers, eating while on the wing and landing only at their nest sites. Some people say they are even able to sleep while they are flying!

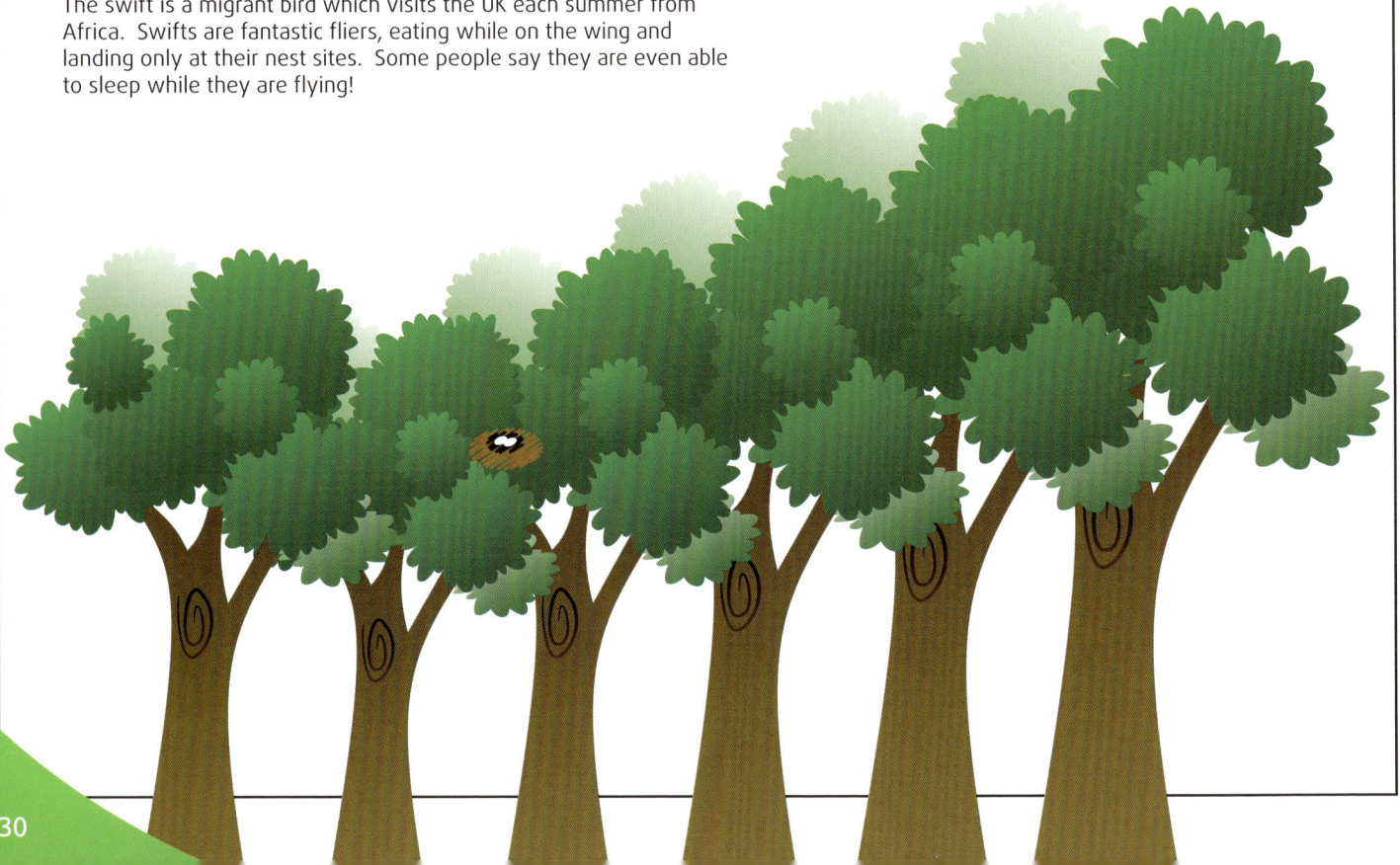

Signs for spring - Vocabulary

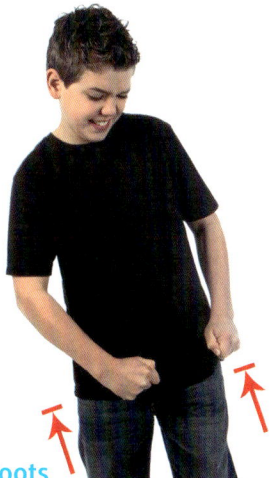

Boots
With both hands in a 'Fist' shape in front of your waist, mime pulling a pair of Wellington boots onto first the right and then the left side.

Bud
Starting from the tip of the left index finger, use the index finger and thumb of the right hand to open and close, describing the outline and shape of a bud.

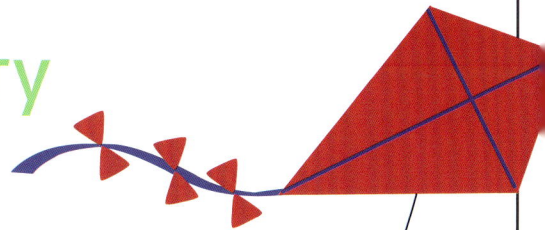

Kite
Both hands made into 'Fists', with the thumbs tucked into bent index fingers, mime holding the string of a kite.
Look up at your imaginary kite and make short tugging movements on the 'string' to show how the kite flies in the wind.

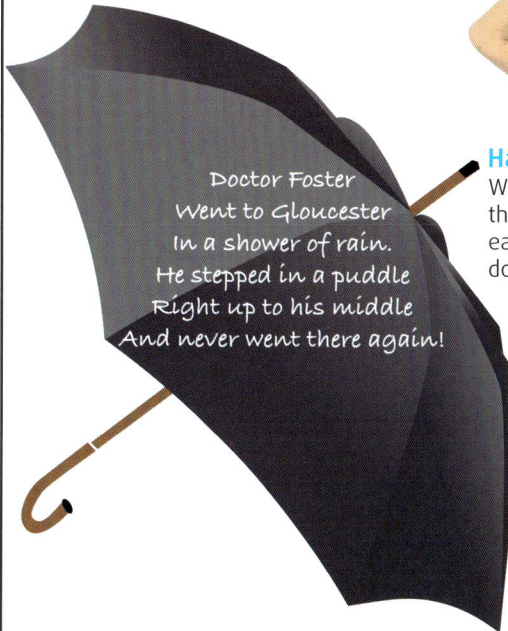

Hat
With the index fingers and thumbs of both hands touching each other, mime pulling a hat down onto your head.

Doctor Foster
Went to Gloucester
In a shower of rain.
He stepped in a puddle
Right up to his middle
And never went there again!

Spring / Bloom / Grow / Plant
Hold a 'Flat' left hand with palm facing back. 'Bunched' right hand moves slowly up behind left as the fingers slowly spread open to show the growth of new things.

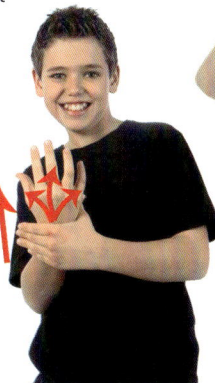

Umbrella
Mime opening an umbrella.

Things to **make** and **do** in **spring**!

There are loads of things to do in spring.

Olli says:
Did you know that kites were originally used in battle—to scare away enemy troops and to send signals?

Make a bat kite!
Follow these simple instructions to make the coolest kite in the sky.

You Will Need:
  · Paper
  · 2 drinking straws (the longer the better)
  · Scissors
  · Coloured pens
  · Some string and sticky tape

Method
1. Using two sheets of plain paper, draw the outline of the wings and body of your bat, (or butterfly if you prefer) on one sheet of paper and the body and head of your bat on the other.
2. The wings of your bat should be about 15 centimetres in height and have a wingspan of about 15 centimetres across.
3. Colour in the wings and body of your bat and give him a funny face!
4. Carefully cut out the wings (Don't forget to make sure that they are still joined in the middle).
5. Cut out the body.
6. Glue the body to the centre of the wings.
7. Make sure that the kite is totally flat and attach the two straws in an 'X' shape across the wings using the sticky tape
8. Next, strengthen both the wing tips with sticky tape.
9. Firmly attach a piece of string about 50 centimetres long to the centre of the 'X' made by the drinking straws
10. Your bat is now ready to take to the skies! You may need a friend to help launch your kite as you hold on tightly to the string and run.

Grow a sunflower!

Sunflowers can brighten up even the dullest day.

With just a little effort you could soon be growing the tallest flower around!

You Will Need:
- Sunflower seeds
- A cardboard egg box
- Cling film
- Multi – purpose compost
- A water mister
- Large plant pots
- Garden canes
- String or garden twine

Method

1. Fill the cardboard egg box with compost and press a single seed into each compartment.
2. Gently spray the compost and seeds with water.
3. Loosely cover the egg box with a sheet of cling film.
4. Put the egg box somewhere where it will get a lot of light, such as a window sill, but make sure that it is not in direct sunlight or the compost could dry out.
5. Keep the compost damp and wait for the seedlings to appear.
6. When your seedlings have two leaves, carefully remove them from the egg box and replant them in large plant pots. Make sure the plant pots have a layer of pebbles at the bottom so that water can drain away easily.
7. As the plants begin to grow taller, push canes into the pots and tie the stem of the plant loosely to them with the string. Don't forget to keep the compost moist!
8. When the weather gets warmer, and there is no danger of frost, you can move the plants outside and either keep them in their pots or plant them in the ground in a sunny spot that is sheltered from the wind.
9. You will need to dig a hole that is at least 50% bigger than your plant pot.
10. Be very careful that you don't damage the roots or the compost around them as you remove the plant from its pot.
11. Once it is in place, carefully fill around the plant with soil and place a very tall bamboo cane behind the plant. Water gently.

Keep the soil damp; especially in dry weather.

Don't forget to measure your sunflower plant every week to see how fast it grows.

When your plant has flowered and died, cut off the head with about 30 cm of the stalk remaining and then tie it with some string or twine to the side of a bird table or branch of a tree as a tasty snack for the birds!

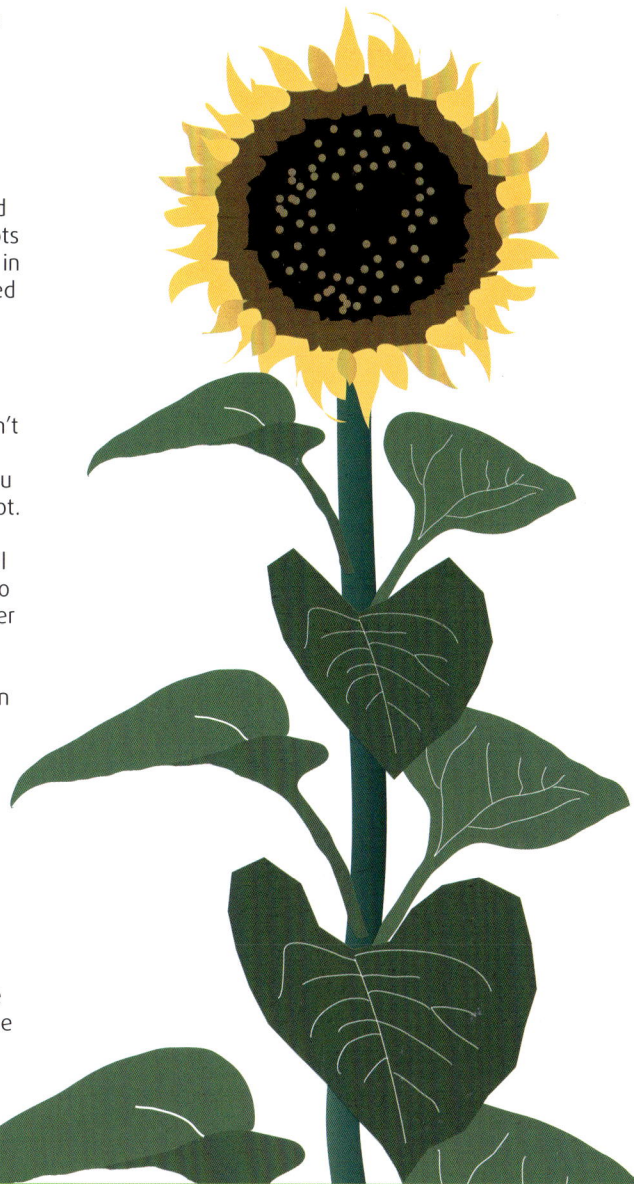

Why Not Also Try:

Grabbing your rain gear and going outside to splash about in the puddles.

Hold out your hand during a shower of rain and try to count the number of raindrops that fall onto the palm of your hand. You will need to be able to count really fast!

While you are outside don't forget to give the air a good sniff. A shower of rain can change the smell of the outdoors – Isn't it a brilliant smell?

Signs of summer

School holidays, ice cream, lemonade and long lazy days – Brilliant!

The long summer evenings mean that wildlife can keep active for longer. Plants are in full bloom and the animals and birds are busy looking after their young.

This is also the time when lots of insects begin to hatch. Insects are amazing creatures with no backbone and six legs. Most of them even have wings too. Summertime is when the insect world really gets active. The air, the water and the ground are literally buzzing with life!

Insects are a great source of food for many animals, but some people eat them too! There are over a million known species of insects throughout the world, so there are enough to keep any hungry animal or person fat and happy...

Anyone for beetle on toast?!

Olli's Forecast

Time to chill and unwind!

By now most of us should be enjoying long, hot, sunny days followed by warm, relaxing evenings.

While you're out having fun, make sure that you protect yourself. Stay out of the sun during the hottest times of the day - between 11am and 3pm. Cover up with a t-shirt and a hat. Wear sunglasses – not only will you look really cool but you will be protecting your eyes too!
Never look directly at the sun because it will damage your eyes.

Don't forget to use a sunscreen with a high UV factor to help protect you from those harmful rays.

Drink plenty of water.

Even though the weather should be mostly sunny, keep your eyes on the skies and check out the clouds.

Look out for fluffy, cotton wool, type clouds with flat bottoms; these are called Cumulus clouds. As long as they are low in the sky the weather should stay fair, but if the tops of the clouds start to grow upwards and end up looking like a giant piece of broccoli then watch out. This type of cloud is known as a Thunderhead, or Cumulonimbus cloud, to give it its proper name.

Whatever you want to call it, this cloud means that it's time to take shelter because rain and thunder could be on the way!

Look Out For:

Things that fly fast.....

Late June and July is a brilliant time for going out to ponds, lakes, streams and wetlands to see dragonflies.

Not only do they look fantastic with their shimmering colours, but as their name suggests, dragonflies are fearsome creatures. They are the number one predators in the world of insects.

A dragonfly can fly backwards just as fast as it can forwards.

Despite their fierce name, the dragonfly doesn't bite or sting and is not dangerous to people.

The largest dragonfly in the UK is called the Emperor Dragonfly. It has an amazingly large wingspan of 10.5cm.

Imagine that if you were a small insect being chased by a dragonfly that big, you would need to be able to move very fast indeed!

Things that fly slowly.....

Another insect sharing the summer skies is the much slower and gentler butterfly.

In the past people used to call them 'Flutter-byes'

While they might not be as fearsome or as fast as a dragonfly, some butterflies are great at making themselves look much more frightening than they actually are. Butterflies, such as the Peacock, have patterns that look like large eyes on their wings to fool predators into thinking that they are much bigger insects.

Butterflies can be crafty too and often lay their eggs on stinging nettles to stop them being eaten by animals.

Some butterflies hibernate, spending the winter in places like sheds and sheltering among plants such as ivy. You can help butterflies to survive the winter by making a pile of logs in a quiet corner of your garden for them to shelter in.

I think our skies must get pretty crowded sometimes, because even though many of the butterflies that we see in the UK during the summer have made their way here from Africa and Europe, there are also over 50 species of British butterflies.

Maybe there is an air traffic control tower somewhere making sure that all those flying insects don't crash into each other!

Olli says:
Did you know that some butterflies only live for a week?

Things that can leap.....

Meanwhile, down on the ground, if you look really carefully you might see a grasshopper.

Grasshoppers are actually quite large insects but they can be difficult to see because they are experts at blending in with their surroundings.

Like many insects, grasshoppers have wings, but usually they get about by jumping with their powerful legs.

A grasshopper's legs are so strong that it can leap up to twenty times its own body length. That's like you being able to jump a distance of 30 metres!

I wish I could jump like that and bounce my way to school everyday!

Signs for summer - Vocabulary

Allergy
Right 'Clawed' hand scratches up and down left forearm as if scratching a rash.

Blackberry (Two part sign)
Sign 'Black' by moving a 'Closed' hand down the side of the cheek and then add the sign for 'Berry'.

Berry
Hold out the index finger of your left hand in front of the body, pointing right to represent a stalk. The fingertips of the right hand, in a full 'O' shape are held against the tip of the 'stalk'. The right hand twists forwards and away in the action of plucking a berry from a stalk.

Pollen (Two part sign)
Finger spell the letter 'P' and then rub the tips of the thumbs and index fingers of both hands together, as if you were rubbing tiny grains of powder through them.

Raspberry (Two part sign)
Make a 'Fist' with index finger extended and slightly bent. Brush the tip of the index finger downwards twice over the lips to make the sign for 'Red' and then sign 'Berry'.

Shorts
Both 'Flat' hands, with the palms facing upwards, tap twice against the upper thighs.

Summer
Draw a 'Flat' hand across your forehead, as if wiping away sweat.

T Shirt
Both 'Flat' hands, with the palms facing upwards, tap twice against the upper arms.

Little Boy Blue come blow your horn,
The sheep's in the meadow the cow's in the corn.
But where is the boy who looks after the sheep?
He's under a haystack fast asleep.

Things to **make** and **do** in summer!

Holidays are here at last - time to chill out!

Make an Olli Egghead!

Not only will you be able to grow some tasty cress, but you'll be able to give me a haircut too.

You Will Need:
- Egg shells
- Compost
- Coloured pens
- Scissors
- Glue or sticky tape
- Packet of cress seeds

Method

Ask an adult to soft boil an egg for you (An egg makes a tasty breakfast!).

After you have scooped out the inside of the egg try to keep as much of the shell in one piece as possible.

Carefully wash out the egg shell.

Photocopy the picture of my face and use the coloured pens to colour it in.

Stick or glue my face picture to the egg shell.

Fill the egg shell 2/3 full with compost and then sprinkle some cress seeds on the top.

Water your Olli Egghead every day and it should start sprouting 'hair' in 2-3 days.

Don't forget to give me a haircut!

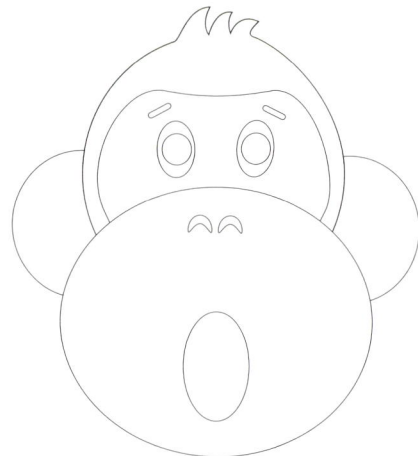

Make lemonade!

My Grandma says that if life gives you lemons then you should make lemonade.

I have no idea what she means, but I do know that this is a great way to chill out on a hot summer afternoon!

You Will Need:
- An adult to help or supervise you
- A saucepan
- A lemon squeezer
- A large jug
- 1 cup of sugar (approx 200g) or less if you don't like your lemonade to be sweet
- 1 cup of water (approx 237ml) to make the syrup
- 1 cup (approx 237ml) of freshly squeezed lemon juice from about 5 or 6 lemons
- 3 or 4 cups (approx 946ml) of cold water
- Ice

Method

Make the syrup by gently heating the cup of water and the sugar together in a saucepan until all the sugar has dissolved.

Let the syrup cool and squeeze the juice from the lemons into the cup, making sure that you take out any pips that may have fallen in.

Add the juice and the syrup to a large jug and top it up with the remaining 3 or 4 cups of water.

Put the jug in a fridge and leave it to chill for about half an hour.

Serve in large glasses with lemon slices and ice.

If you prefer your lemonade to be fizzy, try using sparkling water in place of tap water.

Why Not Also Try:

Organising a treasure hunt for you and your friends.

This is a simple game that can be played almost anywhere with any number of players and, best of all, it costs nothing!

Obviously, you and your friends are not going to be searching for gold and silver coins, but there is a different kind of treasure hidden all around us....

First, decide on where your treasure hunt is going to take place. It might be in your garden, a park or even on a playing field.

Make sure that everybody knows what the boundaries of the hunt area are and if there are any 'no go' areas that might be dangerous, such as ponds or steep hills.

Be sure to tell an adult what you are doing and where you are going.

Next, organise your friends into teams. Give each team a sheet of paper with a list of objects that have to be collected within a set amount of time.

For example, your teams may have as little as fifteen minutes or a couple of hours, to collect as many things as possible from the suggestions below.

When the time is up, the team with the most things from the list wins!

Things to collect might include: something prickly, a pinecone, a leaf from a tree such as an oak or a horse chestnut, a smooth, flat stone, a seed, a feather, something colourful, something to tell the time with, something shiny, something furry, something smelly, a forked twig, a daisy, or a sprig of clover.

If your teams have a camera, you could make the game even more interesting by awarding extra points for the teams that come back with photographs of special things, such as an animal track, a snail, a spider's web or a magpie.

If you don't have a camera, your friends could always draw the items instead.

See what new items you can think of for your friends to collect and record.

Just remember to always leave the environment as you found it and stay safe by following the 'Safari Safety' tips on page 53.

Signs of autumn

Foggy mornings, toffee apples, bonfires and fireworks lighting up the night sky!

Slowly the days are starting to get shorter as summer comes to an end. Overhead, flocks of birds can be seen flying to warmer places for the winter. Suddenly the trees become a dazzling display of red, orange and gold as the leaves change colour before drifting to the ground to form a thick carpet that is just perfect for kicking up into the air on the way to school!

The hedgerows are full of berries, fruits and wild mushrooms, a perfect larder for all those hungry animals and birds getting ready for the long winter.

This is a busy time for squirrels too. Because they don't hibernate, squirrels are very active burying nuts in the ground for them to eat later when food is in short supply during the winter months. The squirrel finds the nuts again using a combination of memory and their strong sense of smell.

Maybe my dad should try using his nose to help him find his car keys when he is late for work in the mornings!

Olli's Forecast

Autumn is a time of change.

One minute I'm lazing in the sun, enjoying my summer holidays and the next the shops are full of signs reminding me that it's time to go 'Back to school'!

In September it can still feel like summer during the day because of the warm sunshine, but at night it can turn a bit chilly. Time to put on your woolly jumpers!

Out in the fields, Farmers are busy ploughing the fields ready for next year. Gardeners are busy too, sweeping up the fallen leaves and making sure that the frost doesn't harm the tender plants.

The bonfires of burning leaves and the November fireworks, make the air smell of smoke.

But all those autumn bonfires can be bad news for hedgehogs. To a hedgehog an unlit bonfire will look like a great place to spend the winter. Always make sure that you have checked your bonfire for our prickly friends before lighting it.

Look Out For:

Things that slither....

In September it is still possible to spot the largest reptile in the UK lying on a grassy bank, soaking up the rays of the autumn sun.

Grass snakes like to live in damp places such as river banks, where they eat a diet of frogs, fish, mice and even small birds.

They are usually greyish green in colour, often with black markings and can grow up to a metre long.

Grass snakes are fantastic swimmers and often hunt underwater, swallowing their prey while it is still alive!

Although they might look a bit frightening, grass snakes are not poisonous. The grass snake is actually quite shy and wary of humans.

Grass snakes don't have very good hearing, but they are very sensitive to ground vibration, such as the tramping of human feet.

If a grass snake is frightened it will usually slither quickly away or sometimes pretend to be dead by rolling over onto its back and allowing its tongue to flop out of its mouth.

Things that spin....

Frosty autumn mornings help to show up the delicate webs that are spun by some of the 650 different kinds of spiders that live in the UK.

The cartwheel shaped webs that you might find in your garden are called 'Orb webs'. The webs are made by the garden spider.

To us the webs are just nice to look at on a frosty morning, but for an insect they are a deadly trap!

After weaving its web, the spider patiently waits for insects like butterflies, flies and wasps to crash into its sticky web. Once the insect is stuck fast, the spider dashes towards its victim and quickly wraps it in sticky silk to stop it from escaping. Finally, its prey is finished off with a bite and injection of deadly venom before being eaten by the hungry spider!

A spider's web might look really delicate but really they are incredibly strong — Spider silk, by weight, is much stronger than steel. It's waterproof and much more elastic. In fact it's the strongest material known to man!

Spiders are clever and don't just use their silk to catch their prey; some of them even use it to fly!

Just like a comic book hero, the spiders climb to the top of a tall plant or tree and shoot out a single strand of silk. The wind catches the silk and carries the spider along with it.

Using this 'ballooning' technique, spiders can travel quite a long way.

What a great way to travel, it certainly beats catching the bus!

Things that are spiky.....

In October and November, hedgehogs start to make their nests for their winter hibernation.

Did you know that hedgehogs are the only spiny mammal found in Britain?

An adult hedgehog may have up to six thousand spines on its body.

These prickly creatures are found all over Britain, even in our towns and cities. Living in parks and wasteland, lots of them even pay a night time visit to our gardens.

Because they will eat pests such as slugs, snails and caterpillars, hedgehogs are known as "the gardener's friend".

Hedgehogs are very nosy animals, always on the lookout for a tasty snack and will try and eat almost anything they come across. Unfortunately, this can cause problems as they can be injured by the rubbish that people leave lying around. Hedgehogs have been found with their heads stuck in tin cans and empty yoghurt pots.

To stop accidents and injuries happening to wildlife, always make sure that litter ends up in the bin where it belongs.

Many people think that hedgehogs are pretty slow creatures, but actually they have quite long legs and can run very quickly. They are also fantastic swimmers and good climbers.

Because they have poor eyesight, a hedgehog will use its sense of smell more than any other sense. As it walks along it constantly sniffs the ground for food. Its nose is so sensitive that it can smell food under an inch of soil.

Our gardens can be great places for hedgehogs, as long as we don't use chemicals for killing pests such as slugs and snails. Slug pellets can be poisonous, not only to slugs, but to hedgehogs too.

If you want a hedgehog to visit your garden, make sure that fresh water is available and allow parts of the garden to get a bit untidy so that minibeasts, which are the main part of a hedgehog's diet, can live in the undergrowth.

You could even try putting out a plate of some tinned dog or cat food for your spiky guests!

Signs for autumn - Vocabulary

Autumn
Hold up your left hand, palm facing forwards and the fingers open, to represent a tree. Move your 'Open' right hand, with palm facing downwards, slowly downwards beside the 'Tree', wiggling your fingers, to show the falling leaves.

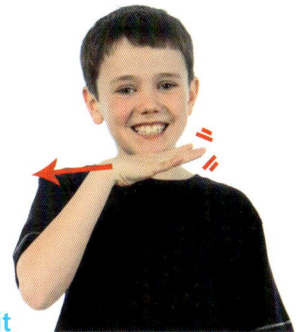

Fruit
Full 'Open' right hand, with wiggling fingers, moves from left to right just below the lips.

Bonfire
Both 'Open' hands, with palms facing each other, move alternately up and down as the fingers wiggle to mimic the flames of a fire.

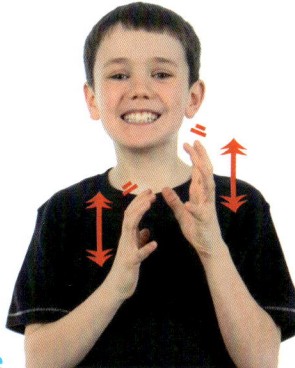

Apple
A full 'C' hand mimes holding an apple in front of the mouth and then twists forwards, at the wrist, as if taking a bite from the 'apple'.

Mushroom
'Clawed' right hand, facing left, twists slightly back and forwards above the 'stalk' of the 'mushroom', symbolised by the extended index finger of the left hand.

Peter, Peter, pumpkin eater, Had a wife and couldn't keep her! He put her in a pumpkin shell, And there he kept her very well!

Scarecrow
Hold both arms out straight at the sides and let your head flop, like a scarecrow.

Things to **make** and **do** in **autumn**!

Take inspiration from the falling leaves and make your very own flying machine!

Make an Olli-copter!

In the sixteenth century, the Italian artist and inventor, Leonardo Da Vinci, drew plans of a fantastic flying machine that many people think inspired the modern helicopter. Perhaps Leonardo got the idea for his machine by watching the seeds from trees like the Sycamore, which spin to the ground like tiny helicopters.

It's easy to make your own Olli-Copter, my version of the helicopter!

You Will Need:
- A sheet of good quality photocopying paper (A4)
- Coloured pens
- Scissors (used under adult supervision)
- A paperclip

Method

1. Photocopy or trace over the template below-right onto the sheet of paper. If you want a larger Olli-Copter, then you can enlarge the template on a photocopier to 150% or 200%.
2. Decorate your copter using the coloured pens.
3. Ask an adult to help you cut out the Olli-Copter and cut along all of the solid lines.
4. Tabs A & B will form the blades of the Copter. Bend blade A towards you and blade B away from you so that the copter looks like the letter 'Y' when looked at from the side.
5. Fold tab C & D behind the back of the 'Olli Copter' lettering and then fold tab E up behind the text too.
6. Attach a paperclip at the bottom of your Olli-copter to give it some weight and to secure tab E.
7. Holding your Olli-copter by the paperclip, raise your arm, then drop your Olli-copter and watch it spin to the ground!

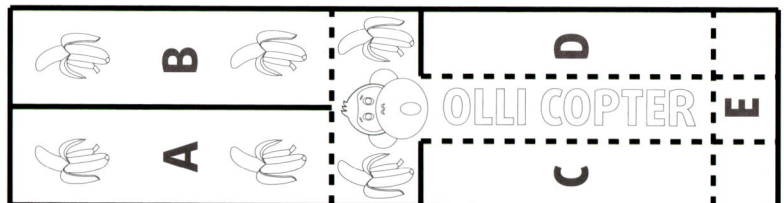

Mini Beast Mayhem!

A beetle drive is a fun and easy game that you and your friends can play using just paper, pencils and dice.

The aim of the game is to be the first player to draw a complete beetle — but the body parts that you can draw are decided by the throw of the dice.

You Will Need
- A six sided dice
- Paper and pencils

How to Play

Each player takes it in turn to roll the dice.

Each number that you roll means that you can draw a different part of the beetle.

The person to have drawn a finished beetle, which has a body, a head, six legs, two wings, two eyes and two antennae, wins the game!

A player needs to roll a six before they can begin.

When you have rolled a six you can draw the body of your beetle and begin the game.

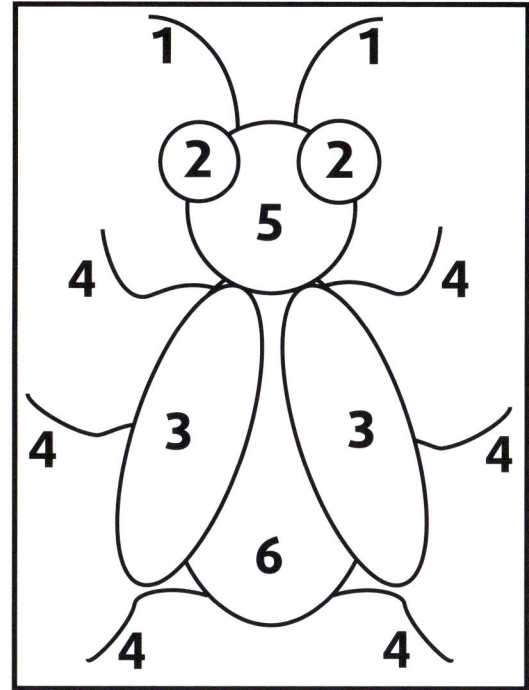

Here are the numbers for the different parts of the body:

6 – Body (you must throw a 6 before you can begin to draw your beetle)
5 – Head
4 – Leg (Your beetle must have six legs so you need to roll a 4 six times)
3 – Wing (Your beetle must have two wings)
2 – Eye (Your beetle must have two eyes)
1 – Antennae (Your beetle must have two antennae)

Why Not Also Try:

Becoming a recycling Rembrandt!

Leonardo Da Vinci and Rembrandt were brilliant artists who used the things they had around them, like paint and clay to make fantastic works of art.
Can you imagine what masterpieces they would be able to create using the things that we throw away every day?

Next time you are sorting out items for the recycling bin, just pause for a minute and try to see things with an artist's eye. What looks like trash to some people is treasure to others!

It might look just like another old cereal packet and a load of old kitchen rolls, ready for the dustbin, to my Grandma.....

but to me it's the beginning of a fairytale castle or even a laser firing robot from outer space!

What does that margarine tub remind you of? Can you think of another use for those old drinking straws from the burger bar?

Signs of winter

Icy pavements, woolly scarves, sledging and making snowmen!

Many birds have flown off to spend the winter in warmer countries.

To survive the cold weather, when food is scarce, some animals, such as hedgehogs, bees, snakes and frogs, find shelter and go into a deep sleep. Their heartbeats and breathing slow down and the temperatures of their bodies drop. This process is called Hibernation.

A hibernating animal lives off their own stored energy until it's time for them to wake up in the spring.

Olli's Forecast

ICE

ICE

ICE

ICE

ICE

ICE

Nature seems to take a nap!

But in fact winter provides an important time of rest and germination.

In the northern hemisphere, December 21st is the shortest day of the year, when the sun at midday reaches its lowest position in the sky.

Expect snow and ice in January.

According to an old weather tradition, St Hilary's Day on January 13th is meant to be the coldest day of the year!

Despite all the dark and miserable days, there is always something to look forward to at this time of year because winter is a time for festivals, such as Christmas and Hanukkah and of course December brings yet more school holidays!

Look Out For:

Things that hoot....

The silent churchyard slept, cloaked with inky darkness. The hands on the spire clock edged slowly around the dial towards midnight, like an ancient spider closing in on its prey.

Suddenly, the silence was pierced by the screech of an owl.....

Ooooh!!! Scary stuff!!!
Every good ghost story needs an owl!

Owls are often associated with the supernatural.

Drawings and pictures of owls have been used by many cultures around the world for centuries. They can be found in the hieroglyphics of ancient Egypt, in cave paintings and of course in ghost stories!

But do they really deserve this spooky reputation?

Perhaps it's because most owls are creatures of the night that they are so often associated with scary stories. But people really don't need to be afraid of owls – it's other birds, insects, reptiles and small mammals, like mice and rats, that need to watch out!

Owls are birds of prey and many of them have special feathers that allow them to fly almost silently, which gives the owl the advantage of surprise.

Owls have fantastic eyesight and can see very clearly when light levels are low.

As well as having good eyesight, owls also have excellent hearing, which helps them to locate their prey. Once an owl has swooped silently down onto its prey, it is able to use its strong feet to capture and grip its struggling victim.

Because they don't have teeth, owls can't chew their prey. Instead they tear it into smaller pieces or swallow it whole. Any bits that their stomachs can't digest, such as bone, feathers or fur, is then brought back up and can be found on the ground as pellets.

Things that rap and tap....

The strange drumming sound that you might hear when you go for a walk in the woods isn't made by a badger playing the bongos!

In fact, it's the sound of a woodpecker using its beak to drill holes in trees. The woodpecker is hunting for bugs hiding underneath the bark. Wood peckers have really strong beaks that can chip holes in the tough bark. Once a hole is made, the woodpecker uses its incredibly long tongue to lap up the insects.

While they are drilling for food, woodpeckers can peck up to 16 times a second.

They also drum on trees to communicate with each other.

With all that drumming it's a wonder that woodpeckers don't always have a headache!

Actually, there's not much chance of that because a woodpecker has special shock absorbing tissue between its skull and its beak to cushion the force of the blow.

Things that bark....

If you hear strange screams or barking during the dark winter nights, it might not be people or a dog making all that noise. It could be a fox.

Winter is the breeding season for foxes. Male foxes are on the lookout for females, and the strange barks and weird screams are their way of finding out who is in the neighbourhood.

The fox, the wolf, the jackal, the dingo and even the dog next door are all members of the canine family. The red fox is the smallest and most widely distributed member of the dog family in the world. It can be found in parts of Europe, America, Africa and Asia.

At first glance a fox might look like a dog and even bark like one. But, if you get close enough you will see, that unlike a dog, the pupils of their eyes are vertical-slits, just like those of a cat.

Despite its unusual eyes, the fox shares other similarities with a domestic dog. The fox is a fantastic hunter, with excellent hearing, and just like some breeds of dog, it can run very fast, at speeds of over 30 miles per hour.

A male fox is called a 'Dog'. A female fox is called a 'Vixen' and a young fox is called a 'cub'. It is the vixen that makes the almost human like screams during the breeding season.

The fox is an omnivorous animal - which means that they are not fussy eaters. Their diet includes mice, rabbits, birds, insects, earthworms, grasshoppers, beetles, blackberries, frogs and fish.

A fox will eat almost anything! They have even been known to eat the flesh of hedgehogs, although they definitely don't eat the skin or prickly bits!

The fox is an amazing animal and is able to adapt to practically any environment, which is why you are just as likely to see a fox scavenging for food in a town as you are in the countryside.

Signs for winter - Vocabulary

Coat
Mime putting on a coat.

Sledge
Both hands in 'Fists', with palms facing each other and thumbs resting on the tops of the index fingers, move up and away from the body and then back in an arc to describe the curved shape of the runners of a sledge.

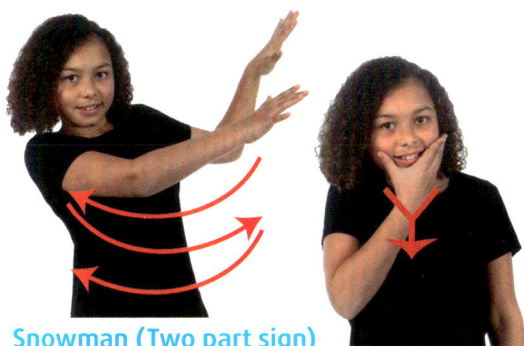

Snowman (Two part sign)
To sign snow, both 'Open' hands, with palms facing down, move slowly downwards and from side to side, with the fingers wiggling to show the gentle fall of snowflakes. Then make the sign for 'Man' by using the fingers and thumb of one hand to stroke down either side of the chin, to show a beard. The fingers close onto the thumb underneath the chin.

Gloves
Mime putting a glove on each hand.

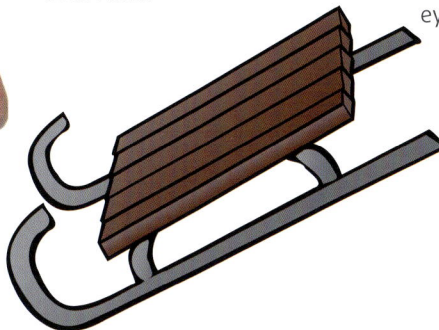

Winter / Cold
With both hands closed at either side of the chest, mime as if you are shivering with the cold.

Hibernate (Two part sign)
First sign 'Cold'. Then sign 'Sleep' by using your thumbs and index fingers of both hands and slowly closing them together at the sides of the eyes to mimic the eyelids closing.

Scarf
Both 'Closed' hands are held at the side of the neck. Cross your arms as if you are putting on a scarf.

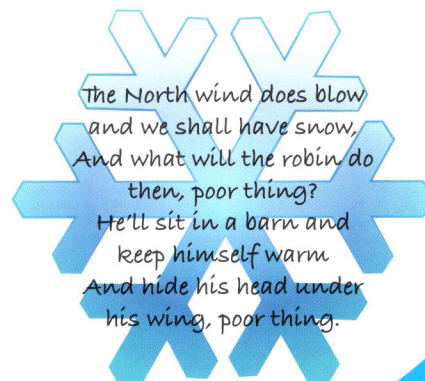

The North wind does blow and we shall have snow,
And what will the robin do then, poor thing?
He'll sit in a barn and keep himself warm
And hide his head under his wing, poor thing.

Things to **make** and **do** in **winter**!

Help the wild birds survive the winter months!

Make a Peanut Butter Bird Banquet!
This is a really quick and easy treat that's sure to be a hit with our feathered friends.

You Will Need:
- Slices of bread
- Crunchy peanut butter or lard
- Wild birdseed or chopped mixed nuts
- A biscuit cutter
- A cocktail stick
- A knife to spread the peanut butter
- String

Method
Use the biscuit cutter to cut out shapes from the slices of bread.

Use the cocktail stick to make a small hole in the bread near the top of your shape.

Thread the string through the hole.

Leave the bread for a few hours to dry out a bit.

Thickly spread the peanut butter onto both sides of the bread and then coat the shape with the chopped nuts or birdseed.

Hang the bread shape from the branches of a tree.

Sit back and watch the feast!

A night out with the stars!

No, this isn't an evening at a glitzy film premiere. It's a chance to get to know some of the stars who have been around a lot longer than those that you see at the movies!

Wrap up warm and spend some time out in the back garden, looking at the night sky. It's a fantastic way to see the stars and more environmentally friendly than flying all the way to Hollywood!

To help with your stargazing, use the internet or get a book from the library to find out what you might expect to see in the night sky.

In Britain, the night sky is at its best during the winter months, as the stars often appear at their brightest on a cold, clear night, even if you live in a big city.

Stars form patterns in the night sky that are called constellations. One of the most famous constellations of stars is known as 'The Plough'. 'The Plough' is easily found lying low in the northern sky during November and December.

On a clear and moonless night we can usually see up to 3,000 stars without a telescope or binoculars. If you use binoculars to look at the stars, you will notice that stars are different colours. Some are white, but others are green, red or blue.

With a bit of research you will soon easily be able to spot some of the planets such as Jupiter and Venus too.

Orion

Ursa Minor

Why Not Also Try:

Rain or Snow....See where they go!

There's no reason why the rain or snow in winter should make you feel glum. In fact, a rain shower or snow can help to bring out the detective in you!

After a downpour, get out a magnifying glass and see how many different animal tracks you can find in the snow or mud.

Anything that walks, runs, hops or slithers should leave a tell tale clue!

Get a nature book from the library and use your detective skills to find out what left the mystery tracks.

Be brave and follow the trail to see where your mystery animal was going.

Maybe you're on the trail of a legendary beast that nobody has ever seen before....

....or possibly it's just next door's dog!

Either way, don't forget to take a photograph of the track, just in case your friends and the local newspaper don't believe you when you tell them that you have discovered a fantastic, new animal!

It's a **wild**, wild **world**!

You don't have to live near a jungle or a rain forest to come into contact with wildlife. Nature is everywhere – even in the streets of our towns and cities!

Many of us are so busy with our daily lives that we often take our surroundings for granted and fail to notice just how much is actually going on around us.

Take time to go out for a walk in the area where you live and pretend that you are an explorer who is visiting the area for the very first time. Have a really good look to see what is around you.

How many different types of plants and animals can you spot?

Look at all the different varieties of plants and trees. If you look closely you are sure to see plants like dandelions, nettles and thistles growing in neglected areas. Many people think of these plants as weeds, but in fact a weed is just a plant that is in the wrong place!

Remember when you are on your safari to look all around you, from the ground to the rooftops. Count the different species of birds that you see. You could even get a book from the library to help you identify the birds. Soon you will be able to tell a starling from a house sparrow!

If you are lucky enough to have a garden, you could put up a bird table or a feeder to attract birds. Even if you don't have a garden, you can still feed the birds by buying a seed holder which can be stuck to a window.

Most villages, towns and cities have a park or even an area of waste land that has been left to grow wild. Why not adopt an area as your own personal nature reserve and see how many different plants and animals you can see there? Check that you are not trespassing on private land and make sure that you have told an adult where you are going.

Try spending an hour observing the area and record what you see in a notebook. You could even take photographs of the insects, plants and birds for your nature journal.

Draw a map of your nature reserve for your notebook. Mark on it any trees, buildings or natural features and colour them in. Make a note of any plants or animals that you have seen and mark their positions on the map with a cross.

The creatures that visit your nature reserve will change not only with the seasons but also with the time of day. Who knows, you may see bats at dusk or even a fox taking an evening stroll!

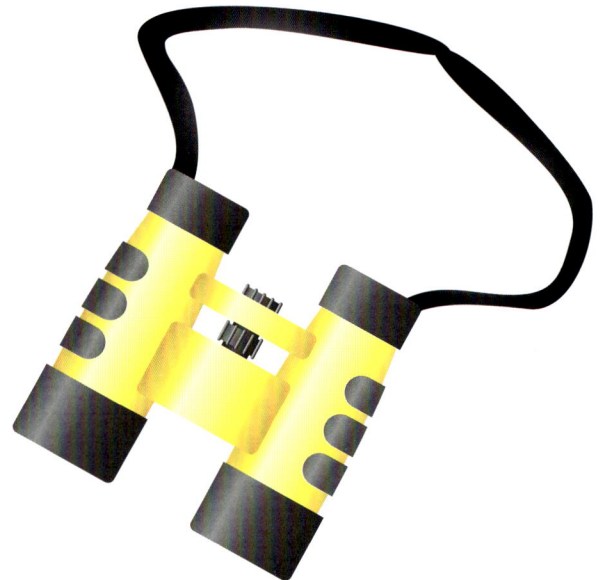

Safari Safety

It's great fun exploring the environment, but there are a few rules and things that you need to know to make sure that you stay safe while you are on your adventure.

- Tell an adult where you are going.
- Go on your safari with a group of friends.
- Make sure you are dressed suitably for the weather.
- Don't do anything that could put you or anyone else in danger.
- Don't pick any wild flowers or plants. Take a photograph instead.
- Take your litter home with you.
- Put logs and rocks back where you found them.
- Stick to footpaths and close any gates.
- Keep your dog on a lead.
- Many berries and fungi can be poisonous. Do not touch them and wash your hands thoroughly after your safari.

Ant / Bug / Insect / Ladybird
'Clawed' hand shape, with wiggling fingers, scuttles away from the body.

Animal
With 'Clawed' hands, palms facing downwards, make small forward movements as though creeping through the undergrowth.

Badger
A full 'C' hand, with fingers pointing downwards, moves over the front of the head, towards the back to indicate the white stripe on a badgers' head.

Bat
Index finger of one hand is pointing outwards horizontally to represent the branch of a tree, whilst the index and middle fingers of the other hand hook over the 'branch' to show how a bat hangs upside down.

Bee / Fly / Wasp
An 'O' shaped hand moves across the body, mimicking the flight of a winged insect.

Bird
Open and close the index finger and the thumb near the mouth, to imitate a bird's beak.

Butterfly / Moth
Both 'Flat' hands are held in front of the body with the palms facing the body and thumbs linked together. Gently 'Flap' the wings of the 'butterfly'.

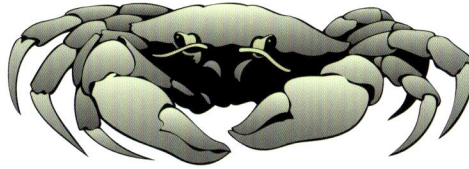

Crab
Open and close the thumbs and fingers of both hands and move them across the body to indicate a crab's pincers, opening and closing as it walks sideways.

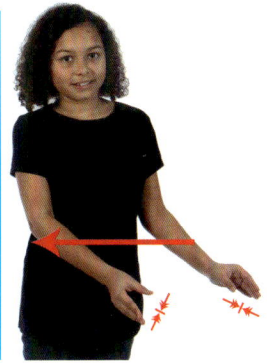

Deer
Both 'Open' hands are held at opposite sides of the head, with palms facing forwards and the thumbs touching the temples. Then move your hands away from your head to show the shape of the antlers.

Dolphin
Slightly bend one hand, with the palm facing downwards and then move it up and down and across the front of your body to mimic the way a swimming dolphin dives in and out of the waves.

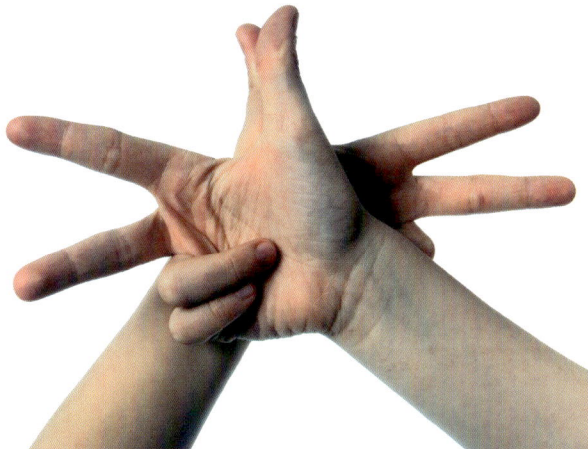

Dragonfly
Extend the thumbs, index and middle fingers of each hand. Place one hand on top of each other, with the palms facing upwards, to show the outline of the body and wings of a dragonfly.

Duck
The fingers of a 'Bunched' hand open and close onto the thumb in front of the chin, miming the beak of a duck opening and closing.

Eagle

Hold a right 'C' shaped hand, with the palm facing to the left, at the tip of your nose. Move it away and downwards in a slight, beak like curve, closing the thumb and index finger together.

Feathers

The index finger and thumb of the right hand move backwards and forwards, opening and closing along the left arm, to show the outlines of feathers on a wing.

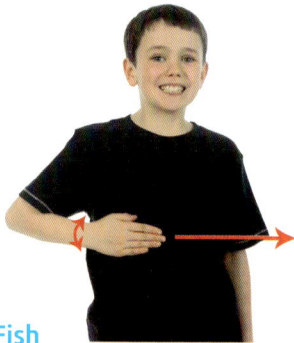

Fish

'Flat' hand moves forward across the body, twisting slightly at the wrist, in a swimming motion.

Fox

Fingers pointing towards the face move away from the nose into a 'Bunched' hand to show the shape of a fox's snout.

Fur

The fingertips of both hands make small opening and closing movements away from and down the body, with the fingertips closing to a 'Bunched' hand to show the fur on the body of an animal.

Frog

Fingers of a 'V' shaped right hand bend and straighten as they make small jumping movements up the left arm to mimic the legs of a hopping frog.

Goose

Open and close the thumb and fingers of a 'Bunched' hand in front of your chin, like a beak opening and closing. Then tilt your hand forwards and downwards, miming the action of a feeding goose.

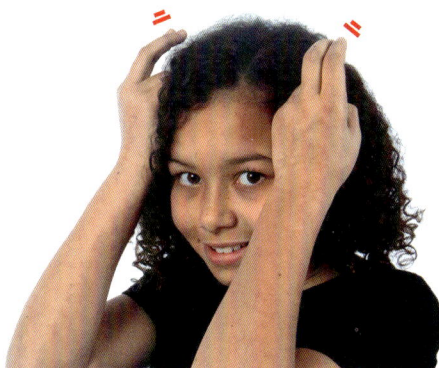

Hare

Hold two 'N' hands at either side of the head, with the palms facing backwards. Show how a hare bends its ears back by bending the fingers back at the knuckles twice.

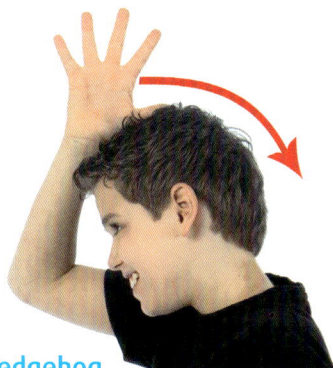

Hedgehog

One 'Open' hand, with fingers splayed, moves backwards across the middle of the head to show the spines of a hedgehog.

Mouse / Rat

Hold the tip of your index finger against the side of your nose and twist your hand quickly backwards and forwards at the wrist.

Owl

Hold your hands in front of your eyes, bending the index, middle fingers and thumbs of both hands and twist them from side to side twice to show the big eyes of an owl.

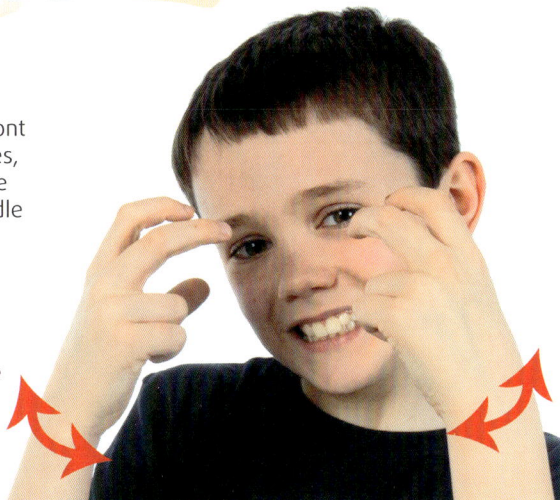

Predator

Hold your left hand in a 'Fist' in front of your body, then move your right 'Clawed' hand towards it, clasping your left fist as if your right hand were the jaws of a biting animal. Make sure that your face has a fierce expression.

Prey (Two part sign)
First sign 'Predator' (P 57), then use your right index finger to point at your left fist to show the animal's prey.

Rabbit
Hold two 'N' hands at either side of the head, with the palms facing forwards. Twitch the 'ears' by bending the fingers at the knuckles twice.

Seal
Both 'Open' hands are held in front of the body so that the backs of the hands are touching each other and the fingers pointing downwards. Wiggle the fingers backwards and forwards.

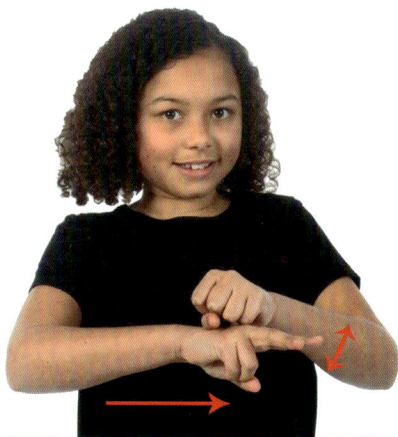

Snail
Make the shell of the snail by making a 'Fist' with your left hand. Hold your right 'V' shaped hand, with the palm facing downwards, underneath the 'shell' made by your left. Flex the index and middle fingers of your right hand to show the 'eyes' of the snail.

Slug / Worm / Caterpillar
Flex your index finger and move it slowly forward to show the wiggling movement of a worm.

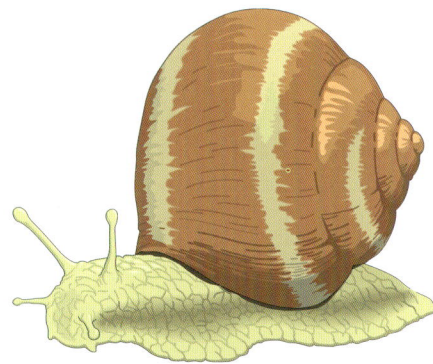

Snake
Hold your hand in a 'Fist' at your mouth, with the knuckles of your fingers facing forward. Flick your index and middle fingers out in a 'V' shape to mimic a snake's forked tongue.

Spider

'Clawed' hand shape, with wiggling fingers, moves downwards from beside the head, like a spider descending by a thread.

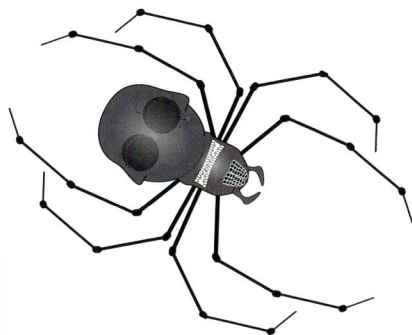

Toad

A 'Full C' hand moves forward from the neck and back, to show the movement of a toads' throat as it breathes.

Squirrel

Starting at the side of your body, use a 'Full C' hand to describe the shape of a squirrel's tail.

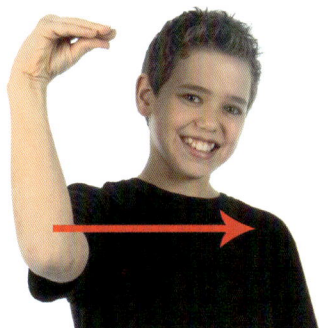

Swan

A 'Bunched' hand, representing the head and neck of the 'swan', is held at head height in front of the body.
Move your arm slowly across the front of your body, as if the 'swan' were swimming past you.

Woodpecker

The tips of the index finger and thumb touch together to form the shape of a beak, then make several short 'pecking' movements back and forwards, as if tapping an object.

Whale

Both 'Flat' hands are held in front of the body, with the palms facing the body and thumbs linked together to show the shape of a whales' tail. Move the hands downwards, as if the whale is diving down into the ocean.

Little Miss Muffet sat on a tuffet eating her curds and whey. Along came a spider, who sat down beside her and frightened Miss Muffet away!

A Jungle in your bedroom!

Sometimes it really is too wet, too cold, or too dark to play outdoors, but just because you are stuck indoors it doesn't mean that you can't still have some fun.

If you can't go outside to see the animals, then the animals will have to come to you!

It sounds amazing, but you have everything you need for your own private zoo on the end of your arms!

Your hands are amazing, they can be used for so many things, such as holding objects and picking things up. Your hands can be used for waving, pointing, and of course, you can even use them for signing with!

But, I bet you didn't know that with a bit of practise you can also use your hands to make the shadows of fantastic wild animals.

It's easy to make shadow animals. All you need are your hands and a torch or lamp. You will also need a plain white or light coloured wall as a background to cast your shadows onto.

Make sure that the room is dark. A single, strong, light behind you works best. Try using a lamp without a lampshade or ask a friend to hold a torch.

Stand between the light and the wall.

The pictures opposite will help get you started. Try to copy the drawings then change them until your shadow looks the way you want it.

You can make the animals larger or smaller by moving back and forwards towards the light. The shadow will get bigger the further away from the wall that you get, but it will also get fuzzier and not look as sharp, so experiment to see what works best.

Try turning your hands slightly to change the way that the shadow looks.

People have been putting on plays and shows for their friends and families for centuries. In fact, making shadows on the wall is such an old form of entertainment that some people think that it started when people still lived in caves!

Perhaps they would gather around the fire at night and entertain each other with stories about the animals that they had been hunting that day, using their hands to cast shadows of the creatures on the cave walls.

I suppose it must have been the caveman version of television!

When you have learnt a few of the animal shapes, why not try making up your own show for your friends featuring your shadow animals.

Your friends are sure to be amazed when you introduce them to the jungle in your bedroom!

Olli says:
Wow! That crocodile is really scary, I'm glad it's only a shadow puppet!

CRAB

CROCODILE

WOODPECKER

BUTTERFLY

SNAIL

Afterword by **Philippa Forrester**

Humans are part of the real world and by that I mean the natural world, yet so often we feel disconnected from it. So much so that we hear of children who live in cities sometimes having no understanding of where their food comes from.

It is so important for us to be close to nature every day because it can give us a sense of meaning and belonging to something. The natural world is our home and only exists as a set of finely balanced relationships. Our children need to understand this concept and how all those relationships work, if we as a human race are to survive on the planet.

If children are to experience the deep joy that being close to nature can create, it is our duty, as parents and carers, to let them out into the natural world to explore and enjoy it under our watchful eyes.

Each new day and new experience acts as a brushstroke on the fresh canvas of a child's brain, some heavy, some light, some brightly coloured, others more subtle but altogether, over the years, creating an individual picture of how that person perceives the real world to be.

It is vital that that picture includes the natural world.

> **It is so important for us to be close to nature every day because it can give us a sense of meaning and belonging to something.**

As a mother, I feel it is part of my job to create new experiences and to expose my children to as much as I can, from the insects under stones in the garden, to the broader experiences of travelling the world.

I try as much as I can to get them outside, and they benefit from fresh air, wild animals that pop up where you least expect them, watching the seasons and learning the names of birds and plants.

We grow our own vegetables together and although time working in the vegetable patch often only amounts to them stealing some raspberries and weeding for five minutes, at least they know where raspberries really come from!

All the time I hope that they are beginning to make connections on their canvas.

I have always felt a passion for the beauty of the natural world; it has been with me since my own childhood and is the reason I did a degree in ecology and conservation.

Being a mother has only intensified my passion and my delight as I share my love of all things wild and natural with my three boys.

I dearly hope that we can all foster in the new generations a sense of wonder and respect for the other plants and animals that share our world and I am sure that this wonderful book will only help.

Philippa
Philippa Forrester, Television Presenter & Broadcaster

About the author...

Garry Slack is a former Communication Support Worker for deaf people and has extensive experience of supporting both deaf and deaf-blind people in many different situations.

Garry has developed and delivered sign language and non verbal communication workshops to people of all ages, including training for parents, children, young people and professionals.

As well as devising the award winning "Learn to sign with Olli" series, Garry is a freelance trainer and speaker on non verbal communication, working in partnership with several local authorities throughout the UK.

When not teaching or writing, Garry lives a quiet life in Lincolnshire with his partner and several noisy sausage dogs!

A big thank you...

I would like to thank all the people who have helped with this project.

Thank you to Nick Baker and Philippa Forrester for their wonderful contributions. Thanks, as ever, to Matt Maddock for taking the fantastic photographs.

Paul Collings, the Youth Theatre Officer for Peterborough City Council and the models, Elliott, Freya, Paris, Sam and their families.

Thanks to Johnny, for his outstanding design and hard work, Cheryl Joyce, from the Forestry Commission at Fineshade Woods in Northamptonshire, for her invaluable advice on animals and a special thank you to the staff at the Royal Society for the Protection of Birds and the Wildlife Trusts, for their help with researching this book.

Whether you are in a town, city or the countryside, if you would like to find out more about where to see wildlife and get involved in events and activities near you, visit

www.wildlifetrusts.org
www.rspb.org.uk

For their belief, support and help with promoting this book, my thanks go to Steve, Lauren, Jane and Charlotte at Action Deafness Books.

actionDEAFNESSBooks

This book is dedicated to the memory of Glenys Walkley, a true friend, who will be greatly missed by all who knew her.

Index of signs